CODEPENDENCY

Why Do You Attract Unhealthy People? No More Falling Into Toxic Relationships. Break The Suffering Cycle And Learn How To Love Again

DAVID LAWSON PHD

TABLE OF CONTENTS

INTRODUCTION

Do you find it difficult to sustain a healthy relationship? Do you feel as if there is too much going on around you, and the people that you love and care about? Do you see their problems and want to help them by any means necessary? Do you feel that your loved ones are being guided by all the wrong people, and that you are better able to solve their problems? Although you feel the need to intervene—the need to convince your loved ones that you have the best solution, these feelings that are compelling you to take concrete action can be resisted. You don't understand why they don't listen to you, and why they sometimes tell you to back off. Why can't they understand that you, and only you, see the big picture, and the optimal solution? Why do they resent you for that? You're only doing what you think is best! You are always there for your loved ones, but your loved ones aren't there for you. You ask yourself, why? Maybe is time for you to read this book and find out.

Being codependent is an extremely difficult emotional state and we will deal with it in this book. Unlike simple dependency, where one person is dependent upon the other, the codependent person is equally dependent upon the person who is dependent on them. As a result, the codependent individual cannot make their own decisions and they require constant emotional support. A codependent person is a dependent person that needs another person to depend on them. That is the problem we will address in this book. Codependency is a serious condition that deserves more attention than it is usually accorded.

This book will bring into focus the paradox of this condition. A dependent person, due to various factors, is an incomplete personality, extremely insecure, and thus paralyzed when faced with the prospect of making a decision or choosing a course of action.

Here is one ordinary example. An electrician, although trained in his craft, can't bring himself to turn on the electricity after installing a switch.

Why? Because he is insecure and simply does not trust himself to turn on the electricity until consulting his colleague. His colleague does not possess greater skills nor superior training, but our electrician needs to hear confirmation that his work is good before he can proceed. So, you see, the problem is that such individuals are insecure and can do nothing without adequate support and confirmation. This problem is not physical, it is mental, and the causes, as we will discuss, are numerous, and either have their roots in early childhood, or result from a trauma experienced later in life.

For the codependent individual, the problem is greater than that of the dependent individual, although frequently given less attention by mental health practitioners, because codependency is a relatively new concept. What exactly is a codependent person?

Codependent or relationship dependency is a recent concept, so it is useful to explain what codependency entails. The codependent person is one that requires another's positive reinforcement, while at the same time, feeling compelled to control the behavior of the person from whom they seek that positive reinforcement. It is a dynamic to which both become accustomed over time. As a consequence of these needs, people in such relationships move away from one another, rather than growing closer. Do you find yourself in this scenario?

Earlier, in the introduction, we explained the principal difference between the codependent person and the classic dependent person. This is of paramount importance, because many people suffer from this condition, and such persons need to understand that their condition is more complex than the classical dependency condition, because it is one that involves interpersonal relationships, which can cause greater emotional damage.

You feel the need to control, consciously or unconsciously, but you also have the feeling that something is wrong because, although you are sincerely trying to help someone, you are being told that you have crossed the line. If you hear that sentiment frequently, please continue to read this book.

It is best to start at the beginning. It is essential to make the right diagnosis. That is the first step, identifying the problem. Another significant step is an acknowledgment of the problem. Many people are inclined to deny the existence of this condition, and this is understandable, because all mental conditions something of a taboo topic and it is not easy for anyone to say "I have a problem". This book is written to help you understand the nature of your condition, and through that understanding, assist you in resolving the problem.

As we said, this is not a condition that affects only the person suffering from codependency, it is a condition that has complex social ramifications as there are always other people involved. That is why this book is not intended exclusively for codependent persons, but also for those who are in this type of relationship, and feel the pressure, but may not understand its cause, much less have the capacity to identify it.

Codependency can be treated, but first you must recognize it. If you feel the need to exert control over another person because their actions do not suit you, even when these actions are not your concern; if you feel that person is "reserved" only for you, and that others are trying to "steal away" that person from you; if you often feel that you are being criticized; and if you constantly feel the need to justify yourself to someone close to you, such as where you were, what you did, or how you behaved in a given situation; and, if you fear how the other person will react, then maybe it's time to learn about a problem known as codependency by reading this book.

In situations where you see a problem on the horizon that you cannot fully understand, and you feel a pressure that you cannot clearly describe, and you feel that something is wrong in your relationship, then this book may be your salvation.

Codependency is a difficult problem because it affects more than one's self. It creates a barrier between the codependent person and the rest of the world. Moreover, it can often be mistaken for classic dependency. In short, it isn't always easy to detect this condition.

Do you have a constant feeling of guilt? I know you do. That guilt has no basis in fact—right? If you ask yourself what is the specific reason for your feelings of guilt, you cannot find a rational answer. You will find the answers you are seeking in this book.

A codependent person often suffers greatly and feels guilty about everything. If they please themselves in any way, they feel guilty. The codependent person has a need to help everyone, and rarely refuses to provide help. Their personal motto is, "I am only good when I am needed." Those who do not suffer from this condition have a different perception with respect to interpersonal relationships. Whereas a codependent person manages to draw the worst from the relationship. Codependents are often rejected, and end up alone, leaving them no choice but to try once more to build a stable relationship with another person. The problem with codependents is that they expect too much, and at some point, they invariably suffer a huge disappointment. A codependent person loves deeply, and they are always ready to sacrifice themselves for their loved ones, in the context of providing them with aid, comfort, and support, but a problem surfaces when these loved ones distance themselves. The codependent *needs* to help, to control, and, in their view, do what they deem best for the other person. This is exactly the point where these relationships fracture, because no one wants that kind of pressure.

Dependency from relationships emotionally "kills" a codependent person, and therein lies the problem. Codependents feel that they are guilty of everything that goes wrong, both in their lives, and in the lives of the people they love. So, if you feel empty, if you see people leaving your life without explanation, and if you feel that they are ungrateful for everything you have done for them, then this book is for you. If you have the feeling that people are not there for you when you need them, that they are not there for you, but you have always been there for them, if you feel that other people are insufficiently grateful for everything you have done for them, if you constantly have relationships that cease to exist, and if you can't keep a friend, then this book is for you.

Of course, you feel unhappy and lost after these events, but the real cause is not the old saw, "bad people, bad times", the cause is the codependent condition from which you suffer. You need a new perspective on the world. You need to look after yourself. You need to stop blaming yourself for everything. Remember that you are not *always* the culprit in a failed relationship.

So, take this book, and start over. Recognize the problem and understand the true source of your dysfunctional relationships. Let this book be your guide. It will reveal the truth regarding your codependent state, and if you pay attention, you can change, have normal friendships and loving relationships, free of guilt, and without feeling that compelling need to be in control.

If someone you care about suffers from codependency, this book will help you to help that person. It could help you rescue your friendship and also the person suffering from codependency.

PART 1

CHAPTER ONE: UNDERSTANDING CODEPENDENCY

Codependent individuals are very difficult to understand. They suffer from complex emotional problems, to which the scientific community largely turns a blind eye. The bulk of the attention is given to dependent persons. It is easier to analyze a "classic" dependent person than a codependent person. The differences are not that large, yet it is difficult to draw an exact parallel—but possible.

You have a problem trying to understand how the world works. You're like the watchmaker who knows how a clock works, but is confounded by the missing part that can't be found to get the clock ticking again.

This book will help you find that missing part.

Codependents display all the characteristics of the classic dependent personality, but codependents carry additional burdens. Many suffered an early childhood trauma, and the development of their personality is incomplete. Low self-esteem, a feeling that something is missing, depression, and an enhanced need for the approval of others, are characteristics of the codependent individual. Problems arise in their relationships because codependents want to please others, want to help, and continuously offer to help. While at first blush, these traits may not seem problematic, one must realize that these desires—to please, to help, to offer help—are obsessive! The sensitivities of these individuals are high, and they want "everything to be good always". They want that for themselves and they want the same for others. As a result, they try to *help* them and *control* them in every situation. This is where things fall apart, because people feel pressured in such circumstances, and that pressure drives them away from the codependent individual.

We know that it's hard for codependents to understand themselves and most reading this will be in some stage of denial, but that's normal. Know that you are not alone. If you notice this behavior in the person you love, read this book in order to help that person.

The codependent person lacks that inner sense of fulfillment. You feel the void inside, right? That inner void is felt constantly, which is why most experts think that the cause of this condition is either genetic or due to trauma in early childhood.

We know that you suffer from within and that you think you are not as worthy as others; you think you are inferior to others. That's why you're trying to create a sense of dependence in others—you think that is the only way you can keep them. Your problems are deep. Your mental state is such that you fail to realize that you are the victim.

I'm going to tell you something here and you need to understand it, and understand it well. Everyone is responsible for their own decisions. This is not to say that you are not to blame for everything that happens. You need to remember that. So, snap out of this wrong-headed notion, and dismiss that sense of responsibility and guilt. Accept that you cannot control all the facets of your life, much less the lives of others.

Codependent persons feel responsible for other people, their choices, their decisions, their behavior, their needs, their wishes, and their feelings. They feel compelled to help others solve their problems. It is impossible for them to set boundaries and say, no.

Learn to say, no. Learn that there are times when you need to turn away from other people's problems, because they are not your problems and you have no obligation to solve them.

You have a difficult time identifying your wants and needs. You try to please others instead of pleasing yourself. You feel insecure or guilty, and when someone helps you, you are overwhelmed with a sense of obligation. You are often angry, feeling underappreciated and exploited. You fancy yourself the victim. Codependents let themselves go; I am sure that is the case with you. You blame yourself for everything. You expect to be perfect—no one is perfect. You feel guilty about having fun or pleasure. Ask yourself, why? Why do you fear rejection? Rejection never killed anyone. You constantly try to prove your worth to others. You relate to people who lack control, and who have a tendency toward addiction. You are attracted to those with an egocentric, narcissistic personality and then you fear of losing control.

You are naive, whether you want to it admit or not. Not everyone is like you. Many people have a stone where their heart should be.

Your biggest mistake is in failing to see that not everyone thinks as you do. Not everyone feels compelled to help others. Most do not care about others at all. That's why you're constantly hurt. Even superheroes don't always manage to save everyone. Why do you think you can save everyone?

You fall for lies, and tend to lie to yourself as well. Don't hide behind lies, face the truth. Making other people the center of your life is not the answer. You must live your own life.

Codependent individuals fear losing the person who makes them happy, subvert their personal lives, lack confidence in their ability to care for themselves, fear speaking directly regarding their needs and wants, often feel hurt, scared, and worried, and fear their own anger even as others display theirs. Codependents rarely openly display their anger (which is not good), because they fear it will tarnish their image in the eyes of others. We say, so what? It is always better to be loved for what you are, than to be loved for what you are not. Codependent individuals either fail to take themselves seriously, or take themselves too seriously. They avoid conflict to maintain appearances, or they place blame on the other person. They are depressed, prone to illness, and overindulge. Although comfortable in sexual relations, in the progressive phase, they can become depressed, isolate themselves, forfeit their daily routine and structure, neglect commitments, and suffer chronic exhaustion. They may also become violent, develop an eating disorder, or acquire an addiction to drugs or alcohol.

Why would you condemn yourself to such a life? You're wasting your life for the sake of others. You have to change that now.

2.1 You have to understand what caused this problem in the first place.

So, what is the root of this condition? How does one begin to understand the nature of a codependent person? Codependents need to acknowledge themselves as victims, because they are. A bad childhood is the most frequent cause of the codependent condition. Neglect and a constant sense of guilt, foisted upon children by irresponsible parents, is the principal reason people suffer from this condition, and research confirms this.

Codependence begins with basic misconceptions regarding one's self, relationships, needs, and sexuality, which result in systematically misguided perceptions.

2.2 You must change the view of the world around you

Codependents develop feelings of worthlessness. They perceive themselves as unloved and undeserving of love. Such perceptions distort their reality, so they refuse to confront problems and shun personal responsibility, often denying their concerns and becoming preoccupied with another person, which leads to their controlling behavior and their tendency to blame others.

A codependent person tries to effect change in the other person. The other person resists, frustrating the ability of the codependent individual to control the situation and the relationship. This reinforces their initial perceptions, and the cycle repeats.

As we stated earlier, the causes of such behaviors and feelings stem from childhood, and are the consequence of parental malfeasance. Examples include inadequate displays of affection, a rigid family atmosphere, controlling parents (one or both), neglect, emotional blackmail, psychological or physical abuse, alcoholism, or drug addiction. The presence of one or more of these factors can be a precursor to the development of codependency. Biological factors, such as neurotransmitter-level disorders can also be causative factors in codependency, or, at the very least, a contributing variable.

2.3 There is always a way out

The complexity of the origin and symptoms of addiction dictates the complexity of the treatment. In the initial stages, the inclusion of pharmacotherapy can help stabilize a person's general mental state. The emphasis is certainly on continuous psychotherapy, because only in this way can deeper and lasting changes of personality be achieved—at the emotional level, behavior, thinking, beliefs, and, most importantly, basic self-image. It is necessary for a person to learn ways of functionally reacting in relationships, to develop spontaneity and independence, to focus on themselves, their desires and goals, to be emotionally literate, to stop taking responsibility for others, and begin taking responsibility for personal choices, emotions, and behaviors. They need to stop feeling like victims for trying to save others, to develop confidence in their thinking and competencies in communication, to learn how to adequately stand up for Themselves through assertive behavior. Finally, the goal is to develop a capacity for closeness that will help them build healthy and functional relationships that can stimulate their further psychological growth.

If your parent was incapable of fulfilling the parental role, you may have taken over the parental role to fill in the gaps. You took care of your parents and/or siblings, paid the bills, cooked the meals, and now, you are repeating this pattern of behavior in your relationships. You may also learn that people who loved you can (or did) hurt you. If your parents abandoned you, lied to you, failed you, it is very likely that you have become distrustful of others and that you tend to believe that the people you love can hurt you. Therefore, through excessive control, you are unknowingly protecting yourself from being hurt again, and this is where you create the emotional gap between yourself and others.

If you grew up with parents who blamed you for everything and if their behavior toward you was such that you began to hide within yourself while doing everything for everyone, then there is a high probability that you developed a codependent condition and became a person who is addicted to relationships that are unhealthy and toxic. That is why you must read this book and start healing, so that you can begin to understand the world and the people around you from a normal perspective.

We want to emphasize that people who suffer from codependency are victims. They should not be condemned; they should be helped. That is why it is important to read this book. If you are a codependent person or someone you care about is a codependent person, it is important to help them and prevent this condition from escalating into severe depression, anxiety, or worse.

CHAPTER TWO: WHAT IS NOT CODEPENDENCY - CODEPENDENCY VS DEPENDENCY

You are insecure about yourself but think you know what is best for others, and that is a problem. Read this chapter carefully and you will be able to understand yourself much better.

This is one of the most important chapters in this book. The difference between a codependent person and a classical dependent person is difficult to see, but the differences are significant. Here, you need to pay attention to all the factors that characterize both conditions. We will clearly show you what codependency is and the twin key elements for distinguishing between these two conditions.

As we said, regarding the classic dependent person, the dependent state is a topic that has received much more attention, while the codependent state has remained in the shadows and is remains under-explored. Even the best psychiatrist can confuse a codependent person with a classic dependent person.

The consequences are great in both conditions, but we can say with certainty that the consequences in codependent persons are greater, and that if left untreated they can escalate to disaster.

In the previous chapter, we wrote about a codependent person and what their characteristics are and now we will discuss the main features of a classic dependent person.

A dependent personality disorder is recognizable by its general pattern of dependence, and the tendency to submit to others, without which submission, such persons believe that they cannot survive. The dependent personality's dominant characteristics are, fear of abandonment, chronic lack of self-esteem, and constant reliance on other people. Below that manifest submission, lies a large amount of aggressiveness that is expressed passively—that is very important. Because these individuals do not allow their aggression to surface, but rather turn it inward, a common symptom is anxiety. This anxiety is often expressed as health concerns—hypochondria. Dependent, obsessive-compulsive and avoidant disorders, belong to the broader group of anxiety disorders.

The person with the dependent personality disorder does not usually recognize the problem. This disorder is more common in women than in men. It is typically recognized in early adulthood. According to statistics, the incidence of this disorder does not exceed 1% in the general population, although it is reported to be even rarer in practice (around 0.6%).

Although psychotherapists believe dependent personality disorder to be easier to treat, effective treatment involves a lot of time and many challenges.

3.1. Dependent personality - clinical description and conceptualization

The trigger for manifestations of addictive behavior typically arise in situations in which a person thinks they will be left to manage themselves or to rely upon themselves. Then severe anxiety ensues, followed by an attempt to allow others to solve their problems. The dependent personality manifests behavior that is obedient, passive, non-assertive, and characterized by a significant lack of self-esteem.

In interpersonal relationships, the dependent personality is recognized by behaviors that manifest their willingness to sacrifice for others, attach to them, and, above all, their expectation that others will take responsibility.

The way a person with this problem thinks, is characterized by suggestiveness, and preoccupation with interpersonal relationships. They tend to think of loved ones as would a constantly worried or overprotective parent.

Anxiety is the dominant feeling, although people with this problem are often shy (or so they seem). Under stress, they respond with depression.

Their temperament, that is, their reactions to this condition are reflected in lower energy levels, fearfulness, and palpable withdrawal during childhood. We would best characterize their temperament as melancholic. Dependent personality is also recognized by a pattern of emotional attachment best described as preoccupied. They are preoccupied with maintaining the emotional connections that represent their security base. This preoccupation is reinforced by the fact that they see themselves in a bad light and view others in a favorable light.

The basic message that people with this condition received from their parents during childhood could be summed up by the phrase "You cannot do this alone". As a result, these individuals began to see themselves as "fine and cultured, but incapable and fragile." Also, the entire pattern of their upbringing has led them to view the world as "a place full of other people who will care for them, because they cannot do for themselves."

One of the most important criteria, against which professionals make a diagnosis of dependent personality, is that they tend to rely on others to take responsibility in all important areas of their lives.

3.2. You are afraid but you don't run away from responsibility easily like a classic dependent person.

Individuals with dependent personality disorder are convinced that they cannot function independently. So, if one significant relationship in their life ends, they will quickly find another that they will be able to rely upon. Most of their energy is dedicated to maintaining relationships with people, without whom, the dependent person believes, they cannot survive.

3.3. Dependent people have difficulty making everyday decisions without advice and reassurance.

The key lies in everyday decisions. If you are planning a significant life change, of course, you will discuss that decision and exchange views with your family and friends. But the dependent personality type faces their everyday decisions from a position of hesitation and fear. They are terrified to make a mistake. They need others to take responsibility for multiple facets of their life.

It is one thing to seek help another person's help, but is entirely another to expect that person to take responsibility for you. People with dependent personalities turn over broad swaths of their lives to others... out of fear. Life's challenges can seem insurmountable and, therefore, make it appear impossible to face them alone.

Have you ever heard a person say "Everyone has the right to their opinion, as long as they agree with mine?" The dependent has a slightly different view: "I have the right to my opinion, as long as it agrees with yours? "An addicted person does not feel worthy enough to express an opinion different from that of the person that they feel they need.

3.4. They struggle to start projects or do things themselves.

Dependent people fear exposure, because others may realize how worthless they are. They fear failure, and weakness. They will avoid failure by taking no initiative. If they believe that a task is doomed to failure, they will not be motivated to take part in it; they will be motivated to avoid it. In short, they will not risk success, because that success threatens their dependence.

3.5. They feel anxious or stressed when they are alone, or when they think they will be alone.

Dependent people often expect the worst. They do not feel competent enough to live their own lives absent other people. Being alone means being unprotected and vulnerable. The thought of being alone and facing the worst of what life can offer, is simply overwhelming. Dependent people believe wholeheartedly in Murphy's Law: If something can go wrong, it will go wrong.

3.6. They take responsibility when bad things happen - otherwise they run away from responsibility

Life is happening; things are happening. Sometimes those things are bad. Dependent people, who do not love themselves or trust themselves, quickly take the blame for those bad things, even if that judgment is unreasonable. They will take the blame for events, circumstances, and for the actions of other people.

3.7. They feel responsible for meeting other people's expectations.

Also, dependent personalities adopt the expectations of the other person as their own. So when a dependent goes wrong, she not only failed to live up to the other person's expectations but failed her own. Each failure reinforces the dependent's warped self-vision.

3.8. They have an increased need for validation and approval from others.

Dependent persons desperately crave confirmation and approval, as alcoholics crave drink or gamblers seek jackpots. When they get confirmation and approval, the planets align and everything is fine within that person's universe, at least until uncertainty knocks once more. Well, any "victory," though desperately brave, is suspected of being a mistake, at best.

3.9. They are incapable of creating or defending personal boundaries.

The only realistic boundary a dependent has, is within the desired relationship. All other personal boundaries are fluid and negotiable, in order to maintain the desired connection. A willingness to negotiate personal boundaries in a relationship creates vulnerability. Some personality types exploit this type of vulnerability. They are too willing to find out how dependent a person is willing to be. And that need is never filled; the dependent cannot provide enough to fulfill it.

So these are some of the main characteristics of dependent personalities. Do you now see how difficult it is to completely separate the two? Both conditions have many similarities. However, we can point to one specific indicator that separates these conditions, and that is aggression.

Yes, you read that right—it's about aggression. It is the first and primary indicator expressed in codependent personalities. In almost 90 percent of cases, aggression is absent in the classic dependent personality. It is the main factor to look for in the codependent personality. I don't mean classical aggression, which is present in almost everyone, but by the robust and frequent attacks of aggression characteristic of codependent personalities. In contrast, dependent personalities, due to lower levels of self-esteem, and their great respect for others, aggression is, if not absent it is hidden. However, this may not always be the case, because psychology is not an exact science and each person is unique.

3.10. More important features of the dependency state

When a child is born, it is completely dependent on the parent/guardian. Rarely does any other creature in nature have that privilege. As a child matures, they become more independent and less fearful of being alone.

Here, we are referring not only to existential needs, but also to emotional needs. The ability to cope with new and challenging emotional situations is very similar to developing other abilities, such as emotional intelligence. A friend told me how "rude" it was for me to tell my daughter that she had to stand up on her own when she fell, and criticized me for not running to her aid.

I would not reconsider my decision. My inner emotions and parenting instincts allowed me to process the information, determine that she had not been hurt, and recognize that she needs to learn to "rise when she falls". From a child's perspective, the world looks a little different than it does when we grow up. When a child falls and scrapes his knee and his Mom says it's okay "you can" stand up, that is different. The child will love for his mom for making him stronger. Feeling your mother's closeness and being able to rely on her warmth, love, and care are very pleasant emotions. But, if mom does it every time, the child gets the message that "mom knows better / mom knows everything", which means "I can't / don't know".

These "rude" moms tell us that life is not always pleasant and that sometimes it will hurt when we fall, but that we must learn to rise. The mom is still at a decent "distance" to respond "in case of an emergency", but at the same time, she tells the child "I believe you can" and when the child rises and sees that he can, well, that's a great feeling. Children are "proud" when they learn to accomplish things on their own.

Overprotective parents take away the opportunity for their children to feel that way, and this is where the development of dependent personality disorder can begin. This diagnosis cannot be made early, because dependence is a normal developmental stage for a child, but if this dependence persists after adolescence, then we can describe that as dependent disorder.

3.11. What do dependent persons look like?

These are people that can never make a decision and shoulder responsibility. They are frequently in dysfunctional relationships where they are often mistreated. Choosing the option is to remain alone is too frightening, so they remain in these dysfunctional relationships for too long, sometimes forever. They have no tolerance for criticism or disapproval, which they associate with rejection. They rarely show initiative, and you get the feeling that there is no respite for them, because they are under constant stress and anxiety.

3.12. Being their friend is not a bad feeling

They experience their happiness solely through the happiness of others, so they do whatever is necessary to make those around them happy. They pay an expensive price for that happiness. They lose their identity. That doesn't sound nice, does it? The fact that they are not aggressive does not mean that they do not feel aggression. Instead they turn their aggressive feelings into passive aggression. This gift with a bow, makes the person they depend on feel helpless and suffocated. It is not always easy to separate those people who sacrifice for the people they love, and those people who have a dependency disorder. Let's say it's a matter of measure, frequency, and intensity.

What these people provoke in their counterpart is the feeling that they need to be taken care of. For example, the mom leading the dependent home to be nurtured when they scratch their palm. It is quite a challenge to resist that cry for help. It is especially difficult to resist if they happen to be one of those individuals who tend to fall into the role of Savior (in terms of transactional psychoanalysis).

Dependent people pay the price for having others take care of them, and that price is obedience and total subordination. None of us are comfortable with a situation where we have to make a difficult decision, take a stand up for ourselves, or, ultimately, defend ourselves, but when they do encounter such situations (which may not have any objective weight at all), panic develops.

3.13. Partnerships

Persons who are "hooked" by a dependent person must provide strength and support for them. The dependent's partner may get the "goods", but they pay a price, because the sympathetic relationship will eventually suffocate them. It is difficult to know where it begins or ends, because the dependent person does everything to avoid being left behind and rejected. Their life is designed and organized in such a way that they will not have to be left alone.

However, if their partner chooses to end the relationship, they quickly find their next host, because it is unbearable for them to be alone. This means that while the relationship lasts, there is excessive closeness—one that is neurotic, because the need for closeness stems from the fear of being left behind, not because they see the person for who they are and accept it. Being close to a partner is, of course, essential and desirable for building a relationship. However, if the partners lose themselves and feel like one person, they risk their relationship.

How do we recognize this in partnerships? If the partnership is excessively idyllic and without any conflict, essentially untested, there is a risk that any conflict could end the relationship, and so it is avoided. When we look at the dynamics of relationships from the outside, all is not as it seems. When / if a conflict does occur, the dynamics are as follows. Partner expresses disagreement about something, or seeks his space. This reinforces the dependent's role as the victim, causing increased anxiety in the partner, who is thinking, "I did everything for you and you want to leave me." As a result, the relationship becomes painful and troublesome.

The problem is that these relationship dynamics are hard to spot. This type of personality selects people who will take care of them in return for their subordination. They demand to be protected instead of seeking solutions. Needing someone, and in turn, receiving gratitude, is not necessarily an unhealthy need. The question is one of whether the relationship is based solely on the need for one side not to be alone and the other side needing someone. The need for one side to be a victim and the other side a lifesaver. The need for one side to depend and the other side to depend on it.

3.14. An addictive disorder in the business world

The impression they make is that they are gentle and pleasant, kind and peaceful, and never come into conflict at any cost. What a colleague of mine would say, "those are the people you feel you want to hug for no rational reason." Not getting into conflicts at work only serves as a prelude to creating dependent relationships. It's hard for bosses to give them a dismissal for obvious reasons.

They will never show initiative, and if forced to enter into something new and challenging, they will sabotage their success in advance. They are never motivated by work; they will be hesitant, and will give up the battle before it even begins. They live with a deep-seated belief that they are inadequate and they rely solely on external protective figures and they rarely hold positions of leadership.

3.15. Combinations with other disorders

Dependent personalities are predisposed to anxiety disorders. Generalized anxiety can develop due to their obsessive concern that they will be left alone. Also, they may suffer panic attacks when left alone in unfamiliar situations, because they believe they will not be able to cope. Expressing anxiety, possibly even panic, serves to keep the supportive person close, and the dependent will continue to receive their protection. This also prevents the dependent from having to take responsibility and be independent. The development of agoraphobia is a common characteristic, as anxiety attacks occur in situations in which the dependent leaves a familiar and supportive environment. Often, hypochondria also develops, and the dependent personality uses this affliction to attract the attention and care of others. They may also suffer from depression, which is a form of self-aggression, that helps them remain in the victim's role. Of course, these disorders are not the exclusive province of dependent personalities.

In combination with their histrionics, passivity can be transmuted into seduction, which serves their need for addiction. When addiction is linked to narcissistic traits, arrogance is somewhat mitigated. In the case of avoidance disorder, the fear of rejection and ridicule is more pronounced, and the need for support, however inadequate, is increased.

3.16. Symptoms and diagnostics

In practice, dependent disorder occurs in 1% or less of the population. Although anyone can find something on this list that applies to them, this does not mean that they have dependent disorder. You need only be concerned if you have all of the following eight symptoms:

1. Difficulties making everyday decisions without the direction, approval, or reassurance of others.
2. The need for others to assume the responsibilities that they themselves should shoulder.
3. A reluctance to disagree with others for fear of condemnation and/or disapproval.
4. An unwillingness to begin any project or task without first gaining the support, assurance, and approval of others.
5. An obsessive, compelling need for support, that the dependent perceives as the means to avoid inconvenience, disapproval or, rejection. The dependent personality will pursue this need without regard to the fact that it may place their support person or persons in harm's way.
6. When lonely, the dependent feels vulnerable, exposed and helpless.
7. When a relationship ends, the dependent personality will immediately seek out a partner with whom to begin a new relationship. They will not engage in any introspection to discern the reasons for the break-up.
8. They have an unhealthy preoccupation with the thought of being left completely alone, that in such circumstances would not be unable to take care of themselves.

So, the dependent personality, is characterized by a compulsive desire for others to take care of them, and the codependent person, has the opposite desire. A codependent person needs to take care of others and, there is another significant difference.

To accurately define the differences between these two states, we must recognize two crucial factors. The first is aggression and inverse desires is the second; In short, I help others - others help me. These are the two principal factors that differentiate these conditions.

3.17. You hide the anger until you explode and you want to help everyone.

In this way you destroy yourself, because you become the victim. You never run out of challenges, which means you are "behind the wheel" all the time. However, other people don't see it that way. Other people only see you imposing your views. Not everyone listens to you. Try to remember that you don't always need to have help. Even when people exit your life, you need to accept this as a normal process. You need to believe in yourself. There are so many people in this world, and each has a unique story. Eventually, you will find someone who suits you, but first, you have to recover from this condition. That will be possible only if you believe in yourself, and you have already made the first step. You know what I'm talking about.

CHAPTER THREE: HOW TO SPOT THE TRAITS OF CODEPENDENCY?

If you still have doubts about this being the right book for you, read this chapter carefully. This chapter will help you resolve any lingering doubts you may have.

Experts agree that there are three basic patterns of codependent behavior. These three patterns that can be easily discerned and are strong indicators that a person is suffering from codependency.

The following list of behaviors will assist you in your self-assessment. They will be of great help to anyone trying to understand what codependency is. The list will also help those who have been in recovery, and need to determine which behaviors still require attention and correction.

- First pattern: Denial

"I have difficulty identifying my feelings. I minimize, alter or deny how I truly feel. I consider myself a selfless person, fully committed to the well-being of others."

- Second pattern: Low self-esteem

"I have trouble making decisions. Everything I think, say or do is rigorously assessed and always falls short. I feel uncomfortable when I receive compliments, awards, or gifts. I never ask others to satisfy my needs or desires. I do not see myself as a worthy human being...worthy of love."

- Third pattern: Compliance

"I realign my personal value system in order to avoid rejection and alienation by others. I am hypersensitive to the feelings of others. I am extremely loyal and remain in situations that I know not to be in my best interests. I often hesitate to express my feelings and opinions if they differ from others. I neglect my interests and hobbies to do for others. I accept sex as a substitute for love."

4.1. Denial

The human mind possesses one surprising, but useless, ability. Our mind has the ability to distort reality to the point it becomes capable of believing that the distorted version of reality is the truth. This should help to explain the meaning of the first sentence of this chapter.

The phenomenon of denial plays a critical role in the formation of bad habits and unhealthy behavior. People deny that they have a problem with alcohol, pills or drugs. The elements of denial are easy to spot: the girlfriend convinces herself that her boyfriend is busy, and so does not return her calls for days; a cancer patient lying in a hospital bed convinces himself that this is just a viral infection, and that he will be discharged in time for the weekend; a man with alcohol addiction negates the real source of his inability to concentrate, stating that it is because he is overburdened with work; a man having a problem with emotional attachments explains that his insecurity in meeting a girlfriend due to his lack of money and that he does not have his own apartment.

As you read the statements above, I know that you will *deny* the possibility of ever succumbing to such dramatic denials—you're far too self-aware. Yet, denial is pervasive; it is present in each of us. It can be very awkward. What is interesting about the function of the psyche, is that it is much easier to recognize denial in another than in one's self. Denial is a strategy we use to avoid dealing with unpleasant realities, and difficult events.

4.2. How do we deal with reality?

I'm sure you hear comments like this one, "I don't have time to deal with that, I'm too busy." We are constantly doing something, going somewhere, cooking, buying something, and planning what to do next. It seems that overwork is becoming the norm, which provides us with another alibi to slip from reality.

People who practice denial as a defense mechanism often use sentence constructions of the type: "I understand I should, but this is not the moment." We have examples like, "I should get a check-up, but I have a backlog of responsibilities at work." Certainly, these reasons can be legitimate, but it is equally possible that they are justifications for distancing ourselves from the things to which we should be paying attention.

Some people respond with anger when they are trapped by the truth. A husband with an alcohol problem is willing to vent his anger at his wife, insulting her, and calling her derogatory names when she demands that he begin treatment.

People are angry when they are displaced a comfortable existence, and forced to confront that which they have worked so hard to avoid. They feel they are under attack, and they quickly counter- attack. Denial, coupled with anger, makes us blind to the truth, blind to the good intentions of others, and blind to seeing our own scars and our own desires.

In our attempt to avoid the truth, we fail to realize how much energy we invest in being unaware, un-seeing, un-feeling, an un-knowing. One thing is certain, "If you don't pay at the bridge, you will pay at the crossroad." When we use our time, energy and will to escape the truth, we draw on our physical, emotional and spiritual resources. Many codependent persons are neck-deep in denial. So if you are reading this and you are avoiding the truth; you can be sure that the truth will catch up to you eventually. No one ever manages to escape the truth. So if you see the signs of denial, don't ignore them.

This pattern of behavior is easy to discern in codependent personalities, and they pretend that they are t doing best they can. But with the symptoms and the patterns of behavior we have just described, you will be able to recognize individuals with this condition. Do you understand now?

4.3. Low self-esteem

People with low levels of self-esteem are always self-righteous. Often, they cannot accept a compliment, because they question the motive behind it.

4.4. The most common symptoms of low self-esteem

- An inability to trust one's own opinion
- Overthinking everything
- Fear of accepting challenges, concerned that they will not be met
- Austerity towards oneself, but indulgence toward others
- Frequent anxiety and emotional restlessness

4.5. Some lesser known symptoms

- Workaholic:

At work, expectations are set. Pressures at work are less challenging than the pressures in private relationships, where everything is less certain. In contrast, work is more peaceful. Meeting expectations at work is easier, because those expectations are well-defined. We frequently see people lacking in confidence shift their attention to work, and invest all their energy into that.

- Too much or too little success

Most of us understand that people with low self-esteem do not achieve the success they should, because they fear the challenge, and fail to fully utilize their talents. However, there is the other extreme. Because they harbor such an intense fear of failure and rejection, they strive constantly to prove their worth.

4.6. What Are the Causes of Low Self Confidence?

In most cases, everything stems from early childhood. Negative experiences lead to low self-esteem later in life. They are:

- Frequent punishment
- Neglect
- Abuse
- Bullying at school
- Lack of praise, warmth, and care
- Belonging to a minority group

Childhood is the period in which we form our "ultimate boundaries" and "rules for life" that determine our path through life. Consequently, early negative experiences will impact the second-round of our development.

4.7. What is the "ultimate limit" and how does it affect your confidence?

I define the "ultimate limit" as how you feel about something, based on your previous experiences. For example, how you felt when you first left home, becomes the ultimate frontier for everything you have left in your life.

When it comes to self-esteem, the limit is defined by how the people we grow up with treated us—the voices of the people who mattered most to us. For example, did they tell you that you 're beautiful or did they make you feel ugly? As a child, were you made to feel worthless? This manner in which those you love treated you as a child affects the way you see yourself and therefore your level of self-confidence.

This pattern is easy to see. This contributes to the symptoms of codependency we've already discussed. Have you found yourself?

4.8. Compliance

Conformity is the compliant behavior of an individual with respect to the norms and expectations of a social group. Such behavior includes agreement with valid, generally accepted, group norms that are typically enforced through peer pressure. In practice, individuals and groups aspire to fully adapt to their environment and behavior that might be regarded as eccentric or unusual by the group. Conformism excludes creativity, leadership, and activism, and opposes change and progress. This term often has a negative connotation in the sense that it implies losing one's independence and self-worth.

People often opt for security within a group—typically, a group of similar age, culture, religion and/or educational background. This is often referred to as group think, a pattern of thinking characterized by self-deception, coerced conformity to group values and ethics, which ignore the pursuit of alternative courses of action. Reluctance to obey is accompanied by the risk of social rejection. Conformity is often associated with adolescents or youth culture, although it strongly affects people of all ages.

While group pressure can have negative manifestations, conformity is usually considered to be a positive. For example, driving on the correct side of the road is a beneficial conformity. With the appropriate influence of the environment, conformity during the early years of childhood enables a person to learn and to adopt the appropriate behaviors necessary for positive interactions and development within society. Conformity influences the formation and maintenance of social norms and allows society to function spontaneously and predictably through self-elimination of behaviors considered opposed to the unwritten norms. In this sense, conformity is a positive force that prevents acts that are disruptive or dangerous to the group, but conformity can be very dangerous if the conformity to the group is counter to the broader norms of society as a whole.

Compliance is an easy pattern to see, because conformists exhibit practically no personality of their own. They can be dangerous to themselves, because they are submissive, and will do anything for a little attention. For the codependent persons, this compliant pattern of behavior is the worst.

Codependents have no limits when it comes to maintaining control. However, they can be spotted quite easily if you combine the pattern with the symptoms.

How many times have you agreed to something you knew to be wrong? Why did you do that? I'll tell you why. Because it's much easier for you to push problems under the rug than it is to deal with them.

But on the other hand, that's why you need control in the relationship. Through that control, you are replacing all that you have accepted but shouldn't have.

CHAPTER FOUR: HIDDEN SIGNS OF CODEPENDENCY

Just as every man has secrets, every condition has secrets. Some signs can act as a guide for you to determine whether this condition exists in you, or may tend to develop.

Codependent conditions can have hidden signs as the condition develops, and there are warning signs that you must not ignore in order to avoid severe consequences.

5.1. Common symptoms of the Codependent condition

Prolonged sadness; chronic lack of will; loss of interest in once-favored activities; feelings of helplessness or hopelessness; feeling trapped in time and space; and feeling empty inside. Is this how you feel?

Of course, possible these signs may be irrelevant, but they may also indicate the development of a codependent condition. This condition is very severe and you must not ignore the signs. The signs may not represent anything serious, but you never know. This condition is almost always a result of early childhood trauma, and many people manage to overcome it. However, some small thing can act as a trigger, unleashing an avalanche of despair, and you don't react quickly and ignore the signs, you may be headed for trouble. No problem in life stays under the rug forever—remember that.

The codependent condition begins, in most cases, with a subtle depression. However, depression can manifest itself in a completely different way than we expect, making it more difficult to detect. These are examples of the least obvious, yet important indicators related to this condition that need to be addressed:

5.2. *Violating behavior and aggression*

Have you ever experienced a sudden onset of anger? Have you ever tossed your cellphone, fisted the wall, or cruelly attacked someone? Depression and aggression are often fellow travelers.

5.3. *Aggression usually serves as a valve to release the deep sadness you feel.*

Depression can be expressed in different ways; both physically and emotionally. For example, feelings of constant sadness, combined with strange behaviors. Depression can find alternate means of manifesting itself. Men often externalize their depression in this way. Psychologists suggest that excessive consumption of alcohol, love affairs, increased aggression, or withdrawal from loved ones can actually be symptoms of depression, and possibly, the onset of a codependent condition. Physical symptoms are characterized by decreased sexual desire, chronic fatigue, insomnia, and changes in eating habits—starvation or overeating, for example.

5.4. *Irritability/Anger*

Sometimes depression manifests as irritability or anger. It is a lesser-known fact that irritability is not only a sign of depression, but may often signal the onset of a codependent condition, especially if it manifests itself in the long-term relationship with a partner or family. Angry moods and unpleasant behaviors are also associated with a codependent onset. Other emotions, such as sadness, shame, or helplessness, are often masked by anger, but anger is an unanticipated emotion in people suffering from a codependent condition.

5.5. *Perfectionism*

You just can't stand the mess at home. This is because you have a mess in your head, so you clean the one that is obvious to you. You do almost everything like that; you strive for perfection in everything. That is compensation for your inability to clean up your emotions.

Numerous research studies over the years have highlighted the correlation between perfectionism and codependency. Codependents feel that to be loved and accepted is possible only if they are perfect. For a perfectionist to make a mistake is a "mortal sin", and the sign of a personal flaw. As a result, these individuals are easily depressed. To counter the fear of failure, and the shame that comes with it, they need to work on their self-esteem, which is difficult. This is why they should see the help of a professional.

5.6. Inability to concentrate

Are you always remembering the right words too late?

Everyone has trouble concentrating from time to time, especially if something is on your mind. But if the issue of concentration affects your work or your relationships—they may be a sign of codependency. Difficulties with concentration difficulties directly impacts how effectively a person functions. This can impede their work, interfere with schooling, and lead to missed tasks or deadlines.

5.7. Extreme guilt

Guilt is a normal feeling. But if you feel guilty about the direction in which the earth spins, that is not a normal. As I said, everyone is responsible for their own decisions. And you can't stop someone you love from making mistakes. You're not a superhero, and even if you were, the superhero doesn't always succeed in catching the villain—right?

Although guilt is a natural emotion, a deep sense of guilt in too many facets of your life can signal that codependency is developing. Psychotherapists call it pathological guilt. Guilt is pervasive for codependents. They scan the past and see only a series of failures. A codependent person can feel guilty for myriad reasons—for their birth, for being depressed, for not achieving an important role in life— everything engenders feelings of regret and guilt.

5.8. *Moving from sadness to happiness and vice versa*

Frequent, though short-lived switches, from states of sadness to states of happiness, and vice versa, can be a telltale sign that something more serious is occurring. When you are depressed, a joyful event can snap you out of it, and things may seem fine, but only for a short time. Then the depression returns, uninvited, and for no apparent reason. Psychotherapists cite this as an "interesting" symptom of depression, in which someone temporarily "rises" from their depression, because of a positive event, opportunity, or interpersonal relationship. It is briefly alleviated, but soon, they return to a depressed state.

5.9. *Self-healing by the wrong methods*

I know you suffer but never try to "drown your sadness in alcohol," for example, or to do self-medicate by any means.

This is not such a subtle symptom, but it is worth mentioning. The codependent person often carries addictive behavior as a fellow traveler. People with a codependent condition are more likely to drink alcohol, smoke, suffer from eating disorders, and other addictions. It is important to note that they may become depressed, because they sense that they are losing control. When you are depressed, it is natural to use the tools at your disposal to deal with the condition. The problem is that people don't usually choose the proper tools. It's much easier to smoke or drink than to go to psychotherapy or exercise. The former will make the depression gloomier and allow you to develop the condition, while the latter will allow you to recover. If you find yourself engaging in any type of substance abuse or you change your lifestyle for the worst, seriously consider consulting an expert.

While in many cases the symptoms are highly visible, there are also cases where the person is unaware that they are beginning to develop codependency.

"Mostly, thoughts and behaviors cause significant stress and anxiety," says psychiatrist Dr. Kashmir Rastomji. "However, in some cases, it may be a pattern that is so normal and common for someone that the person does not even recognize the signs of the disorder. Also, stigmatization is often why people do not seek help."

In the early stages, the codependent disorder is difficult to diagnose if a person has other mental health problems—anxiety, depression, and bipolar disorder—because the symptoms often overlap.

Of course, the diagnosis must be made by an expert, but it may be helpful to re-examine your thoughts and behaviors. Here are some things you may be doing that signal you have this condition without even realizing it.

5.10. You do every task to perfection

If even when doing something for yourself, you struggle to complete the task to perfection— a sign of the codependent state.

"We often think of such individuals as ambitious, but the compulsion to achieve perfection can be a sign of codependency," says psychologist Dr. Joshua Klapov.

5.11. Do you make different lists and reminders?

If your time is filled with making lists and notes, and if you are afraid of forgetting something, it is possible that you are suffering from codependency. These may signal that you are trying to achieve control over the situation.

"We consider people like this organized and we think they just want to make sure the work is done," says Dr. Klapov. "But the obsession with thinking that they might forget something, and the compulsion to write it down so they don't forget can grow into a vicious circle, where more time is spent writing than performing the tasks. This could be an important indicator that this is a codependent person", says Dr. Klapov.

5.12. You are cleaning your space often

Codependent disorder means you not only feel that you have to do the cleaning, but that you also fear what may happen if you do not complete that commitment. If you are cleaning your space, not because you want it to be clean, but rather because you fear chaos, it may be a sign of codependency onset.

"An obsessive fear of clutter in the home or space that is unpredictable leads to the rearrangement of furniture, clothing and everything in the home to keep everything nice and serve a purpose," explains Dr. Klapov. But lurking in the shadows may be an obsession that will later manifest itself in a certain individual and a specific connection with that individual.

If you are constantly organizing and reorganizing things around the house, it would not be a bad idea to speak to an expert.

5.13. You check everything twice

Double-checking is a common symptom that many fail to notice they have. If you check everything two or three times, to make sure you have done everything you need to do, you should consult an expert to see if there is the possibility that a codependent condition may be developing.

5.14. Make sure everything is symmetrical

Symmetry in the space you live in can be very aesthetically pleasing, but if you spend your time arranging everything to be symmetrical, even in other people's homes, it can be a combination of an obsessive-compulsive disorder and a codependent state in its early stages.

5.15. You endlessly re-think situations

Alright, most of us have had head-spinning experiences. However, if you cannot overcome a situation, and re-think it over and over, when you are alone, it can be a sign that your need for control is evolving.

"People suffering from this disorder can sit alone and rethink a particular situation, talk or interaction, or they can practice for an upcoming situation over and over," says psychiatrist Prakash Masand. If thinking about something prevents you from participating normally in your daily activities, see your doctor.

5.16. You need constant reassurance

The unrestrained "buzzing" of thoughts is a common symptom of the codependency condition in its early stages. If, when you are alone, you cannot "turn off" your thoughts, you may suffer from this disorder. If you cannot halt your thoughts without inviting friends/family to distract you, seek professional help.

These symptoms do not necessarily prove you have the disorder, but it is certainly important to know that you need not have live under such stress, and that an expert can help you.

CHAPTER FIVE: THE DIFFERENT FACES
OF CODEPENDENCY – TYPES

The human mind has always been an enigma. The condition you have may be one of several types, and you need to learn what your "type" is. This will help you to focus your recovery on that specific type. This chapter will help you as much as the watchmaker's tale at the beginning of this book. You need to find the missing part of the clock. This is the only way your clock will begin ticking again.

There are different types of codependent disorders and it follows there are different types of codependent persons. This is a very important chapter because you need to understand that this condition occurs in different forms. Codependency can take many forms.

It is helpful that you have learned what the patterns of codependent person are, and that you know the symptoms of this condition. However, there variations of this condition, which is why this chapter is important.

What all codependent conditions have in common, are the consequences, and they can be devastating, so it is important to see the range of this condition.

According to most studies, there are three basic types of codependent persons. It's almost the same as a behavior pattern. The three basic types of codependent persons are, 1) the codependent addicted person, 2) the codependent abusive person, and 3) the codependent timid person.

1. Codependent addiction - Once codependence exists, it generates the dynamics of betrayal. You are convinced of your partner's love for you. When you learn the truth, you will feel, in some sense, betrayed. There may be lying, false promises, threats and everything else that results from dysfunctional communications. You will begin to provide an accommodation for the manifestation of

another person in the relationship to preserve some sense of control. Over time, these adjustments will become a progressively unhealthy form of relating to someone. You can lose yourself in this vicious circle and not know what is happening.

2. Codependent abuse - When abuse is involved in a relationship, it engenders a disproportionate controlling factor into the relationship as well. The abuse is typically sporadic, so you think "This is not always bad." But you are wrong. Interpersonal interactions are shaped in a manner designed to pacify the offending codependent person. This results in progressively shallow relationships.

3. Codependent fear - Codependent persons will always feel fear, irrational of course but there, nonetheless. This form of codependency is marked by a tremendous lack of self-confidence, and is rooted in the ethics and beliefs of the codependent. This manifestation of codependency is frequently exacerbated by peer pressure, and feelings of insecurity. Codependent individuals will live their lives to please others, because they are in constant fear of losing the other person in the relationship.

These three codependent types always end the same—broken relationships and tremendous emotional suffering.

Codependency is a form of addiction, relationship addiction, so we will refer to it hereafter as an addiction. How painful and dangerous can emotional addiction be? Relationship addicts regard their desperate need for someone as a measure of true love. A disconnection for these emotionally unstable individuals, means endangering their identity, integrity, and personality.

Have you ever loved someone to the point of becoming addicted to that love? Have you ever so wanted to love that you couldn't control your emotions and surrendered to them? Although love is the most beautiful feeling, it can also be painful and devastating, not unlike a vice.

That is what it's like that for those who depend on it, and who do everything and anything to avoid being alone. Codependents may remain in a relationship for months, even years, in spite of the fact that they do not feel good about the relationship. It's as if you think you see, but you actually don't, or when you think you love, but you don't love at all. This is codependency—all kinds of love, for partner or friend—it matters not.

6.1. Being too busy doesn't mean you will never meet the right person

Recent research has shown that relationship dependence is the most common type of dependency in the modern age. The reason, experts say, is the modern way of life, in which there less free time for socializing and making new acquaintances. As a result, people are increasingly afraid of being left alone. Consequently, the codependent individual clings to each relationship vigorously.

For example, it is quite possible to be in passionate love with an unhealthy codependent individual. However, when a relationship is not based on healthy love, understanding, and mutual respect, the relationship develops into a painful and devastating one. Codependent people will break ties, suffer, and become depressed. They blame their partner for everything that went wrong. But you must be honest with yourself, was it all your partner's fault?

Some unhealthy relationships also end up in marriage or cohabitation, and they torment one another for the remainder of their lives. All three types of codependent people are the same when it comes to consequences, so, it is very important that you spot the problem before is too late.

6.2. Who are relationship addicts and how do they perceive the relationship?

People who are relationship dependent desperately seek love, and a partner who will always be by their side, and complete them. In stable emotional relationships, there is no needs based component, which means that it is possible to love someone regardless of what needs and desires are met or not met. Nor is there an obsessive need for the partner's constant physical presence. People who are addicted to relationships do not have an intrinsic connection to their loved one, but instead, define true love in terms of how desperately *they* need that person in their life. Regard it is a warning when you hear someone say, "I can't live without you", or "I would die without you". Codependency compels its victims to do many destructive and self-destructive things, largely to prevent the pain they would feel upon separation or, because they hate the partner they dependent upon, or both.

Loving someone doesn't mean that you own them. In a relationship where you constantly demand your partner to justify their whereabouts, no one will be happy. Remember, it usually better to let them off the leash. I believe that everything happens for a reason. You need to restore your self-confidence, and practice introspection. Remember just one more thing—if you don't respect yourself you will never gain the respect of others. Humans, like other animals, have a sixth sense—fear. They can feel it in you.

Addiction is synonymous with a desire for partner control, mainly manifested in possessiveness, which results in following, spying, or forbidding the partner to work. The codependent may also withhold any information that they believe may threaten the relationship. Nevertheless, these relationships are difficult to leave. It sounds paradoxical. It is preferable to accept the loss of a relationship than to struggle with someone who has a codependent condition.

6.3. When does relationship dependence arise?

The predisposition to future addiction is created very early—around the age of three. To establish our future emotional stability, our early relationship with our mother must comprehend her physical and psychological availability, her role as a "constant" in our lives, and the quality of her interactions. If these needs are met, the child can absorb their mother's positive image, and mirror it later in life. This solid foundation enables the child to distance itself from the mother, leave the nest, so to speak. This is only possible because of the emotional stability provided to the child in their formative years. The child does not feel powerless or abandoned, and they learn the ability to be alone, and to have fun when they're alone. However, this ability is guaranteed to last a lifetime. It is often tested in various stages of our lives.

Experts tell us that this emotional addiction is heavily influenced by the romantic fantasies of love we encounter in books, music, and movies.

Do romantic stories affect addiction? Do the authors of such works lack emotional stability in their creative expressions? As they say, art imitates life. Unstable individuals may build fantasies that are fueled by the descriptions they encounter in works of art. They may act upon them, assuming that these are normal relationships. They may expect that idyllic love is possible, or that pain and suffering does not exist— only "they lived happily ever after." Life is not a fairytale, but codependent people rely on these fantasies, because they do not have a healthy perspective on interpersonal relationships.

Were you aware that the brothers Grimm, who authored countless fairytales, found their inspiration in horror stories and medieval myths? Many of those stories did not originally have happy endings, they were re-written with happy endings. As I said, life is not a fairytale.

What characterizes individuals who experience relationships in this way, and how do they behave with regard to the partner?

Allow me to illustrate this behavior through this example. *For fear of being left behind, the girl began to scour her boyfriend's letters, Facebook and messages. She was doing so discretely, knowing that he would be angry, and leave her if he found out. When the boyfriend discovered her treachery, the girl friend displayed none of that fear. On the contrary, as a defensive reaction, she counterattacked, displayed anger, cried, and accused him of being unfaithful. Protesting that she would never do something like that, and that he had made her act that way, which of course was simply not true. She would not do that if he was a man who could be trusted.* When they lack confidence in a loved one to remain faithful, when they face solitude as a result of their partner leaving, they are motivated to control him in a covert, violent way. They will do anything to avoid being left behind. If they believe they cannot live without this person, isn't it logical that for them to do everything possible to keep them? But just because it's logical, doesn't mean that the phrase "I can't live without you," should be taken literally. That is not normal behavior. Would you want to be that girl?

Psychologists tell us that such relationships are difficult to recognize, because many people interpret such behavior as normal and acceptable.

The truth is that many fail to recognize that they are in an interdependent, unhealthy relationship. However, some do recognize it for what it is, but cannot, or will not admit it to others, or to themselves. If they admit it, then they might be forced to make changes. They are extremely reluctant to do anything because uncertainty and separation anxiety. So, their adopted philosophy is, "better any connection than no connection."

Why would anyone choose a relationship they don't enjoy from a fear of being alone? It's often said that a good divorce is better than a bad marriage. However, this is out of the question for the codependent, who cannot feel whole without them, because they serve as an extension of them. They feel as though they would fall apart without them. If such a relationship is broken, the inability to move on is a sure sign that the loss will not be accepted. Emotionally unstable and dependent people who lose their loved one's despair for years, and live for the day to come when they will, once again, find bliss with their partner. This fantasy, along with self-denial regarding taking blame for their partner's departure, leads them to the belief that "everything will be good."

6.4. Can relationship addiction be dangerous?

Relationship addiction goes hand in glove with other addictions. Drug addicts, for example, do not feel emotionally stable, lack control, and need something to complete them—in this case, drugs. Opiate addicts often report that they are complacent, and need no one. This is because the drug fills their emptiness. If one is codependent, then the partner is the drug, hence the statement "I cannot live without you." Relationship addiction can be very dangerous. For an emotionally unstable person, disconnecting means compromising one's identity, integrity, and personality. Such a person is prepared to execute various manipulations to prevent the connection from being broken.

6.5. How can this vicious love cycle be broken, or can this type of addiction be cured?

Emotional stability is something that is built over time and maintained. Those who succeed in doing that have no concerns regarding the "vicious circle." Codependent individuals repeat the same patterns in all their relationships, continuing the vicious circle. Although friends and a supportive environment can be helpful, few can overcome their addictive behavior on their own, and then, psychotherapy is beneficial. In such situations, the client-therapist builds those abilities that the client failed to sufficiently develop as a child. It is a certain kind of "re-education" or "corrective emotional experience." The codependent, in some way, needs to be reborn.

They need to hit the reset button, and learn about the world and about relationships again—this time, in the right way. Believe me, it can be done and you will finally heal and be able to live a normal life in which people do not run away from you.

So, whatever type of codependent person you have a relationship with or, if you are that person, all these indicators of a dysfunctional relationship will materialize and, it is incumbent upon you to see, with the help of these examples, whether you are at risk or whether you are, in fact, a person that suffers from codependency.

CHAPTER SIX: WHICH ARE THE CAUSES OF CODEPENDENCY – DEEP ROOTS

I can say with certainty that we are living in a time of "renaissance" in the field of human psychology. Countless books have been written and extensive research has been undertaken, some of which would not have been possible without today's technology, but we are still just scratching the surface.

The human mind is so complex that no matter how much we research; we will always be at a new beginning. Any illness or condition of a psychic nature is always an enigma. In psychic conditions, new questions are constantly asked, which usually leads to a fresh set of questions. Psychic conditions are, at their core, extraordinarily complex and extremely difficult to understand. No matter how answers the experts give us, there will always be new questions.

Earlier, I noted that codependency is a relatively new term. It was first recorded, relative to other psychic conditions, in 1941. While other psychic conditions have been studied for centuries, and receive much attention, codependency is still barely explored. However, this emotional state and its roots can be found, as is often the case with many conditions—in early childhood.

7.1. *The deep roots of codependency*

Did we come to the question of why? I know, so that you have been reading and you have been patiently waiting for the answer to why "your watch is not working" and what is that missing part? You will find your answers here. After you find all the answers, you can finally begin to assemble that watch, and it will start to tick again.

The deep roots of codependency are typically the result of early child-hood trauma or, in very rare cases, genetic predisposition.

In relationships, friendships, and ordinary day-to-day interpersonal re-lationships, it is very important to find a *yardstick* to measure the manner in which we seek and receive emotions, closeness, and intimacy. Emotional dependence, or excessive attachment can be a big problem in relationships.

Research shows that anyone can be addicted, and not only in love rela-tionships. Addiction can occur in a variety of relationships, parental, and so on. We can become dependent on our children, parents, relationship partner, best friend, or work colleagues—basically to any social construct. Interdependence in our interpersonal relationships can make it difficult for us to establish stable relationships with others, feel contentment.

Love, in male-female relationships, is often displaced by dependence on the other person, without whom, one's own life seems empty, meaning-less, or worthless. What does a codependent relationship look like? What drives us to give ourselves to give infinitely to loved ones, or to demand something unconditionally? The crux of the addiction is the erroneous be-lief that "I can't stand being without them." Bonding in an immature way, by completely surrendering yourself to a partner, leads to addictive love. This type of relationship occurs when one believes that they cannot func-tion without the other. This brand of love is marked by sacrifice, self-pity, and passivity. The only pleasure codependent person can experience, comes from their partner's affection and emotional response.

7.2. Affection without limits

There are myriad unhealthy reasons why people stay together. On the psychological side, people who are preoccupied with their relationship are characterized by a negative image of themselves and a positive image of others. We call that that, partner idealization. We call the party who fears rejection, a codependent person. They ignore their own feelings, needs, and wants, and instead, focus on the feelings, needs and wants of their partner, their friend etc.

Partner dependence is far from harmless, often causing the same physical and psychological consequences as other addictions, psychiatrists claim. We may be emotionally and unrelentingly attached to certain people in our lives, but this is an immature form of connection. Such behavior can make life difficult in all its aspects and foster unhealthy relationships, which can rarely survive.

The common trigger for that addiction, is a paralyzing fear of losing love and support, the fear of loneliness that is deeply hidden in the subconscious, and the constant search for guarantees that cannot be given. At first glance, addicts appear calm and gentle, but hiding beneath that façade is a person who views themselves as helpless, and who fear taking any initiative. Not only does this type of personality seek support in difficult situations, but they also require someone to rely on for the most routine of decisions, while, paradoxically, feeling the need to control them. Over time, partnerships are marked by endless anxiety, and panic over the possibility of losing control. They easily fall into a vicious circle, gradually losing touch with their environment, their friends, and their family.

7.3. Basic characteristics

Codependent personality traits are not always clearly identifiable. Emotionally dependent persons are characterized by preoccupation with relationships; excessive need for closeness; the desire for total unity; social and emotional isolation; remaining in relationships for fear of being alone; easily falling in love; idealize their partner and new relationship; a rapid and intense start into relationships. Their characteristic feelings in codependent relationships are anger, passion, jealousy and an obsessive need for control. Do you understand the issue here?

Codependent personalities *always* need to control the other person in the relationship. There is always possessiveness; unrealistic fears of being left behind; a sense powerlessness, and helplessness when left to themselves; and an inability to express grievances of any kind. The relationship becomes a maelstrom of stress, depression, guilt, and regret. And the biggest cause is a bad childhood.

7.4. Formation of trauma

You may or may not remember, but close your eyes and think deeply about why you such emptiness. Remembering why will serve you well, because, but for that *why*, this problem wouldn't exist. Close your eyes and try to recall how you felt in your childhood. Somewhere in the past lies the core of your problem. You experienced trauma, and now we must see what that trauma was, and how it has manifested itself in later life. In this way, you can return to the moment when your watch was broken. Now, it's up to you to find that missing part.

As we've said before, the formation of addictive behaviors may be the result of some childhood trauma, or parents' overly critical attitudes. Usually, these people were raised by overly strict parents, or parents who placed conditions on their love: For example, they might say, "I don't love you because you weren't good." When such a child grows up, they see that image of themselves in the eyes of others, especially those they are close to, as in a relationship or marriage. Unsure of their value, they strive to keep their partner by their side. This invariably leads to the deterioration of the relationship, and usually to its end. As many as 80 percent of young women and 60 percent of young men believe that it is better to stay in any relationship than to be alone—they believe that the meaning of their life is contained in a partnership. That is a frightening statistic.

7.5. Childhood

As children, most codependents relied on their parents, grandparents, or older siblings. Most were obedient children who accepted advice and the opinions their parents imposed upon them. As children, they did not have the opportunity to make their own decisions or undertake responsibilities. They were not permitted to make their own decisions, and so they were deprived of experiencing the frustration and tension that is inherent in the decision making process, and this is responsible for creating that feeling of emptiness. Another possible scenario is the pre-codependent child confronting their parents, and creating drama around every decision or choice.

Everyone must be involved in the dilemmas and the problems, whether it is buying shoes, choosing a school, getting married—family, friends, neighbors...*everyone* must be involved. Then there are codependents who practice a substitution strategy, replacing the family relationship with a relationship to their chosen partner.

7.6. Meaning

All children are entitled to a good start in life. We know that the experiences that children gain in their earliest childhood have a tremendous impact later in life. New developments in neuroscience tell us that the infancy through six years' stage of life is crucial, as the cerebellum grows and more 1,000 brain cells connect every second. These changes directly and indirectly define the child's health, capacity for learning, future success and, ultimately, future happiness. This development is taking place at this stage of the child's life and cannot be recreated at some point in the future. This is why it is so very critical.

Experts in neuroscience assure us that early childhood development is the future of the modern world. They explain that recent brain research indicates that the early years, from birth to eight years, and prenatal development (before birth) are periods of heightened sensitivity to the development of brain capacity. This means that there is a period when it is "most desirable to encourage the development of certain capabilities and functions."

For example, neuroscience tells us that the period of heightened sensitivity for the formation of basic brain architecture is before birth, and for the development of emotional control from six months to the second year (previously it was thought that this period began in the second year). Also, science has shifted the period of heightened sensitivity to the development of symbolic thinking to the age of 18 months, which significantly changes the view of regarding the importance of play for a child of that age, and the need for adult participation in organized support for development and learning.

This is unambiguous evidence that investing in early childhood development is the cornerstone of societal progress. To paraphrase the old adage, "the first years last forever" has been proven to be true, because their impact persists throughout the child's life.

It is also the period of greatest sensitivity. If the child is not offered a developmental environment, but instead experiences neglect, violence, poor family relationships, exposure to either overwhelming or inadequate stimuli, a rigid upbringing, an unstructured upbringing, a lack of emotional support, poverty, isolation, and/or discrimination, the will be at risk for the onset of developmental disabilities, and personality disorders, one of which is codependency.

7.7. *Those years*

In early childhood, children build the neurological and psychological foundations for the future, and it is very important that the pillars be strong and stable, so that it can bear the burden of the abundant superstructure needed for lifelong physical, social, & emotional health, and academic, and economic success.

7.8. *Parents*

Parents represent the first human contact and communication in a child's life. They are the child's most important teachers. Parents must pay attention their needs, to learn to interpret and recognize the child's signals, sent by voice, gestures, and gaze. Parents must respond positively to these signals. The child needs to feel welcome in this world, and feel that their environment is safe, as these are the conditions for successful learning. That's why a child needs, from day one, a smile on a familiar face, touching, pampering, kissing, hugging, swinging, singing, and talking. Children need stimuli in their environment, such as colorful pictures, mobiles, interesting objects, etc. Interacting with the child through play, reading, coloring, games and other activities is crucial to healthy development.

A child that is raised in a colorless environment of negative emotions, passivity, loneliness, and limited interaction with its environment, does not develop the same number of brain synapses and neural connections as the child who is exposed to various positive stimuli. Learning and memory capacities are stunted. The absence of stimulation during periods of heightened sensitivity to development in later years (beyond the age of eight) can be offset by increased activity (e.g. learning), but much more effort must be made by the individual, family, and community. How successful a child will be, in any field, depends largely on the quality of their early development, the extent to which the brain's potential was enhanced by positive stimuli, the relationships built in the family, the family atmosphere (supportive or overwhelming), and whether or not the child was respected as a person, and accepted & supported by unconditional love, so as to develop in the direction of his natural capacities and interests.

7.9. It all starts with trauma

Trauma is defined as an existential threat or overwhelming situation that surpasses one's ability to cope. An event that triggers a traumatic reaction is beyond the ordinary human experience and poses a threat to one's own life (earthquakes, wars, refugees, illnesses, injuries, loved ones' loss, traffic accidents, etc.). A traumatic event breaks down common response systems that give people a sense of control, connection, and meaning. Common reactions to trauma are intense fear, helplessness, loss of control, and fear for one's life. Children are also exposed to traumatic events. However, their psycho-physical make-up and limited life experience, necessarily means that children face trauma differently. To an infant, the world is their mom. Through her, the world is decoded, as dangerous and scary, or as motivational and supportive. In the event of exposure to a traumatic event, an infant will instinctively become alert, and rely on their evaluation of the parental signal. The child's subsequent reactions will be based on its understanding of the signals sent by the mother, or other parental figure. A supportive and competent mother can make the world a comfortable place for her baby even when circumstances are not the best. It is equally true, that a mother overwhelmed by her own fears, even though in fairly decent life circumstances, can send her child a dark picture of the world.

A child who has acquired solid cognitive-emotional competencies, is more likely to enjoy a good life than a child who has not.

Hypothetico-deductive scientific models are increasingly being used to explain the occurrence of codependency.

Researchers tell us that separation from family is possible both because of the increased psychic autonomy of the adolescent and the broader psycho-social support system formed through peer friendships. These are important resources for developing psychic activity.

On the other hand, those suffering the psychological consequences of childhood traumatic experiences are encouraged to seek out professional help.

Maybe you will remember and maybe you won't, but I want you to close your eyes and think deeply about why you feel emptiness. Remembering will certainly serve you well, because, absent that trauma, this problem wouldn't exist. So, close your eyes, and try to remember how you felt in childhood. Somewhere in your past is the root of your problem. You have experienced trauma, and now we must determine the nature and scope of that trauma, in order to understand how the trauma has manifested itself. In this way, you will be able to return to the moment when your watch was broken, and find that missing part.

7.10. Let's talk about the trauma a bit more

Trauma is defined as the mental consequence of one or more serious, negative external events, which leave a person temporarily helpless, destroying previously successful defense mechanisms and coping strategies. The "kick", so to speak, is always external, and it causes several mental changes that persist over a long period. There are four characteristics most childhood traumas have in common, regardless of whether a person is diagnosed with codependency or, another disorder in adulthood. Trauma is expressed in one of the following four ways: 1) visually, or through other senses, 2) repetitive behavior, 3) fears related to trauma, and 4) altered attitudes toward people, life, and the future.

Trauma related dreams or nightmares are an almost obligatory component of trauma in adults, but are not often seen in children, especially those under 5 years of age.

1) The tendency to relive the traumatic experience, often triggered when encountering a circumstance or an event the reminds one of the trauma. However, it can occur at any time, during school hours, before falling asleep, during play, or other activities.

2) Through play or behavioral reconstruction of events, aspects of a horrific event are repeated. Post-traumatic play, which a child perceives as fun, is a gloomy, long-lasting and particularly addictive form of repetition. Children are often unaware that their behavior or bodily reactions is trauma related, that they are, in fact, a repetition of thoughts or responses to the sudden shock they experienced. These repetitions can be so persistent and time-consuming that they can become a permanent aspect of their personality.

3) Specific fears, stemming from trauma, are relatively easy to identify, once we understand the nature of the trauma the child has experienced. The specificity and literal nature of these fears are *differentia specifica* from neurotic phobic or anxiety fears. For example, a neurotic child will be frightened of all dogs, but a child suffering from trauma, only of a Rottweiler, the breed that attacked them, and caused the trauma.

4) In traumatized victims, limitations with respect to time perspectives are particularly striking. Non-traumatized adolescents express nearly unlimited ideas regarding their futures, while traumatized adolescents express a desire to live in the moment. Traumatized pre- adolescents rarely speak of the time when they will grow up.

Instead, they express their fear that more terrible things will happen. Their belief in themselves and others is shaken, and "basic trust" is broken. Traumatized children and adolescents view the future as terrifying.

7.11. Childhood trauma

Depersonalization and spontaneous self-hypnosis are important consequences of the repeated horrors that traumatized children have endured. As victims of this ongoing terror, they believe that there will be other terrible events to come. As a result of these expectations, they protect themselves through dissociation. In this way, they may fall prey to codependency. These are common findings in abused children. Some of these children, spontaneously master the technique of hypnosis on their own. This mechanism allows the child a mental escape.

Symptoms of traumatic disorder in children usually begin within three months of the traumatic event, although they may be delayed for months, even years, depending on the individual. Symptoms generally involve some form of recurrence, avoidance, or over-sensitivity and may vary over time. On average, one-half of patients fully recover within three months, and the duration of symptoms in the remaining one-half may persist a year or more beyond the traumatic event. For younger children, relief often comes in the form of repetitive play. For example, a child involved in a serious car accident will repeat their traumatic experience by crashing their toy cars together.

Because it can be difficult for children to talk about diminished interest in important activities, symptoms should be carefully evaluated through reports from parents, teachers, and other adults significant in the child's life.

The neglected child will become distrustful and develop mechanisms that dominate or control the situation. This need for control may grow over time and they too will fall prey to codependency.

Whether you remember being traumatized or not, you can be certain that this is the core cause of your condition. All of us are trying to compensate for something. For example, parents may try to accomplish their unrealized goals through their children. And they push their children because they are compensating though them. Do you see where I am going with this? You are also trying to compensate. However, you compensate through obsessive control, because you are lost that little part of your watch due to the trauma you experienced. But you will get better; don't doubt that for a second.

As we have established, trauma plays the most important role in the development of codependency. If, as a child, you experienced trauma in the clinical sense that we have described, and you are experiencing   the symptoms we have described, then there is a high probability that you will, unfortunately, become a codependent person.

CHAPTER SEVEN: HOW TO DIAGNOSE IT

Making the correct diagnosis is the first step to healing and returning to a normal life. You have absorbed a great deal of knowledge in the previous chapters. You've had the opportunity to learn about the nature of this condition, its elements, and its symptoms.

Now it is time for you to end your denial. Dismiss the denial phase immediately. You now know your real self. You see the truth that has been hidden from you for a very long time. That's great. Now it is time to rely on yourself, not others.

It is time to accept responsibility, and stop running away from the truth. Now you must be brave, because this is your fight. This is a fight you have to win alone. Others may be around you, but it's not their fight, it's yours. They can help you, but only incidentally. The only ones in the arena are you and this condition.

You have acknowledged that you have a problem that is the first step towards healing.

This is the most important sentence for you in this chapter. ***Your diagnosis should be made by an expert.*** So, a psychiatrist is a must. Most do not want to see a specialist. Most fear being stigmatized by others.

Don't be frightened and don't feel ashamed. I know, that throughout your life, you have sought the encouragement of others. I understand that seeking psychiatric help is, unfortunately, a social taboo. However, you need to ask yourself one question—how do you feel now? Are you a happy person? Of course, you're not, and without diagnosis and treatment, you will never be a happy person.

For the first time in your life, stand up for yourself, and seek professional help. Don't concern yourself with what others may think. You must fight for yourself. Remember, you have always been your own best friend and your own worst enemy. Be a friend to yourself, for once in your life.

Don't make the of using the Internet or, chancing some type of self-treatment. Many people make this mistake, and the consequences are dire. I am going to show you some of the biggest mistakes people made regarding their illness.

Almost every codependent person with Internet access has searched for symptoms on Google least once occasion, and, the most frequent result is panic. Why? Because a symptom search usually ends with the conclusion that the condition is incurable. That's wrong! Your condition is curable, but only with professional help.

8.1. The biggest mistakes

To avoid inaccurate diagnoses, I will provide you a few tips.

- Never make a diagnosis for yourself

It is very dangerous to make a self-diagnosis based on Internet searches. Spending time on the Internet will only delay going to the doctor and getting a proper diagnosis. Read this book, which provides you with sufficient information regarding the codependent condition.

- Do not "prescribe" medications for yourself

It is one thing to seek advice for healthy eating on the Internet, but quite another to apply questionable remedies to the treatment of specific diseases.

- Blog Search

Just because someone has a popular blog, it does not mean that they know what they are writing about.

- Contact your doctor

Researching the Internet will make you more anxious, but it won't cure you. You need to see a doctor for a specific diagnosis and treatment.

- Once again—avoid the Internet

Nothing you read on the Internet should be taken as a personalized medical diagnosis. Not even when written by experts. Seeing a doctor is the only smart choice.

When people have a health problem, they often seek an easier, cheaper, and faster path to the information they need, so rather than going to a doctor, they turn to the internet—there is no solution on the internet, believe me. This can be very dangerous. According to a survey conducted in the UK, showed 25 percent of those receiving their diagnosis by consulting Google, received the wrong diagnosis, hence, the wrong treatment.

Dr. Google has become the first stop on the road to healing, but experts warn that people should never make a diagnosis for themselves, as information found on the Internet is often confusing or unreliable.

If you search for your symptoms on the Internet, make your own diagnosis, and determine your own therapy, you only going to worsen your condition.

Delaying a doctor visit only prolongs the agony. surveys reveal many people who admit that they spent days worrying about a problem before reaching out to a doctor, one- third of respondents acknowledge delaying their doctor visit for more than two weeks. Every twentieth patient postponed their doctor for a few years before they sought professional help.

Doctors the world over are confronted with patients who must be persuaded that they do not have the disease Google suggested they had. Physicians warn that online diagnoses do patients far more harm than good.

So forget about self-healing and the Internet. You already know your symptoms, and so it's the time to see a doctor. You will tell him your symptoms, he will make the right diagnosis, and you will start taking medication and going to psychotherapy. After that, the world will be a whole new place for you, trust me.

PART 2

CHAPTER ONE: LEARN HOW TO CONTROL THE EMOTIONS

You've already learned a lot. If you've already started psychotherapy—congratulations. However, you still have a long ahead. This condition requires a great deal of work and self-investment.

Your emotions will not change overnight. It just doesn't work that way.

Emotions are a strong force and you can't simply divert them. If I told you it was possible to turn them off, I would be lying. Emotions are like a river. The course of the river may be changed over time, and that is what you are being asked to do—to divert the river, to make a new riverbed.

Is this possible? Of course! The point is that it takes time. When I told you to press the reset button, I meant for you to change your view of the world around you, not to change your emotions. For emotions, it takes time to change. Maybe you will never manage to change your emotions entirely, but you will learn how to redirect them and control them. The most important thing is for you to change your perception of the world and the people around you. That takes much less time. You will continue to feel all that you felt before, but with help, you will learn how to control your emotions. Until you divert the river...you can build a dam and slow the river's flow.

Practicing emotional intelligence can help you successfully control your emotions, but it also affects the way you deal with stress and tension at work. By remaining constructive, focused and compassionate, you can build relationships that will thrive.

These are the three steps.

- Listen to your emotions and be self-aware

Learn how *you* function. Understanding yourself makes it easier for you to understand others. So, focus on yourself.

- Be authentic

People respond positively to people that are comfortable in their own skin. People acknowledge this honesty, they will identify with you, and you will easily gain their trust. Accept who and what you are. Believe me, those famous words, "the truth will set you free" are not meaningless.

- Observe

Recognize the burdens in your environment and try to resolve them. Plan in advance, and be prepared to react. Refrain from intervening in the problems of others, and don't be too quick to offer your help to others. Remember what I said earlier, everyone is responsible for their own decisions. Don't give any advice at all. You must resist that urge, that little voice that tells you everyone needs salvation, and that only you can provide it.

9.1. How to learn to control your emotions?

Controlling one's emotions requires identifying, managing, and responding to them in a manner that allows them to become useful aspects of our inner experience. Controlling emotions is one of 28 transversal skills that can help you rebuild yourself. Controlling your emotions does not mean that you should ignore, *or* amplify them.

You need to understand that no emotion is an enemy, neither anger nor fear, nor is it sadness. There is no bad emotion just as there is no good emotion. Emotions only determine if you feel better or if you feel worse.

9.2. The way we respond to emotions is always a subjective experience

For example, when angry, you may behave inappropriately toward someone. In contrast, when angry, you may be motivated to fight for yourself, or defend yourself. You can easily see how subjective the emotion of anger can be...sometimes a force for evil, at other times a force for good.

Self-awareness allows you to become a cognitive observer, and become more receptive to your inner feelings. When your emotions seem confusing, overwhelming or paralyzing, they cannot serve you well.

I'll show you a great exercise that will help you control your emotions.

9.3. Dialectical behavioral therapy: Controlling emotions 101

This therapy is easy to follow, and with a little practice, you can learn the skill of managing your emotions. These are the following steps:

1. Understanding your emotions.

Distance your emotional experiences, think in terms of an out-of- body experience. Examine and describe what you are feeling. Don't go for the emotions right away, but instead, take a sensible and prudent pause between feeling and reaction. Pay attention to your experiences.

This may sound like a simple concept, but it isn't. What role do emotions play in your life? Honestly, evaluate your understanding of your emotional experiences. Imagine how much your life can change for the better if you analyze your emotional experiences.

2. Accept your feelings and do not hide them.

The more you choose, consciously or unconsciously, to avoid your emotions, the more likely they are to hurt when you face them later. They will be waiting for you just around the bend. That is why you must be honest with yourself, and acknowledge them. It may be painful, but relief will follow.

If you convince yourself that your emotions are unacceptable or scary, you will succumb to the natural tendency to avoid them at all costs.

3. Use no stress methods.

Try substituting one reaction for another. A substitute reaction can distract you from the previously unfavorable reaction. to an incentive. It is helpful to learn this technique when facing unpleasant emotional experiences that may result from fear, anxiety, anger, guilt, or shame. By actively practicing this relaxation technique, you will be reducing knee-jerk reactions, known to be the frequent companion of unpleasant emotions.

4. Enhance positive experiences.

You've heard the adage; you are what you eat. Try applying it to your inner psychological experience from a different paradigm, you are what you think or, you are what you do.

Focusing on negative, sad, unpleasant thoughts, or behaviors will do you no good. Just as we can create an intense inner state of sadness, so can we create an inner state of peace. Actively direct your thoughts and actions toward positive and healthy endeavors. Express gratitude for everything you experience, good or bad.

Additionally, you should talk to a friend or partner, or take a walk, or take a bath, or listen to soothing music, or you write down the things you are grateful for in your journal.

5. Be mentally present in the moment.

If your thoughts are in the present, your attachment to the past will loosen. Mindfulness allows you to be fully in the present moment. In this way, you can detach from your traumatic past.

Often, concerns about the past or the future distract us from the present moment to a point that we begin to feel that we are not in touch with ourselves. This is why it is important to connect with your inner self and be mentally present in the present moment. Regardless of how intense or unpleasant the emotions of the present moment may be, time will pass. Remember, emotional experiences are temporary. Become a conscious and curious observer of your experiences and you will notice that you have a new connection with your emotions. They have no magical power over you.

6. Be aware of your triggers.

Learning to effectively control our emotions requires regular exercise. Know that when you have mastered them, you will feel like you are the "captain of your ship" and you will realize that everything was worth the effort. Explore your triggers and try to avoid them. Emotions will not take over your life or interfere with your when you learn to understand them, and to manage and respond to them more effectively.

Become aware of what situations trigger certain emotional responses in you. By increasing your knowledge of yourself in this way, you will be prepared to confidently control your emotions during times of conflict, regardless of the situation. Most parents do not teach their children how to effectively identify and manage their emotions, and when these skills are not learned in childhood and adolescence, they grow up to face emotional confusion and sadness in adulthood. The present moment is the only time you can learn to use your emotions constructively. This is accomplished by monitoring and analyzing the emotions related to the experience you have underwent. With these techniques, you will control the emotions that surge within you—the river will be diverted.

CHAPTER TWO: WHO CAN HELP YOU?

As I've explained, this is your battle. You need to rely on yourself. As a result of your codependent condition, you have driven a good number of people out of your life. But as I told you...the past is the past, and the future is in your hands. The watchmaker does not call on anyone to help him. He is skilled enough to repair the watch himself. Believe it or not, you are skilled enough to start repairing your watch yourself.

Of course, this does not mean that other people cannot help you, such as friends, partners, and family. If you examine your situation with a clear eye, you will realize that it is a result of your insecurity and your lack of self-confidence. However, you're still here, and looking for help. The fact that you are reading this book means you're a fighter. Reading this book means that you have never given up on yourself, that you want to improve yourself and that you want to be a better person—both for yourself and for others. It means that you didn't let fear win. It means that regardless of your fears you are fighting back. That means you're brave.

I will show you a few things that you can only learn when you stop relying on others, and start relying on yourself. You need to help yourself first.

- Things you learn when you have no one to rely upon

1. You will learn that although you can try to explain something to someone, they only understand it when it happens to them.
2. You will begin to realize that at the end of the day, only you can help yourself.
3. It is easier not to talk about things because, then you subconsciously expect it to happen, and you get frustrated when it doesn't happen.

4. You will learn who really cares and who just pretends to care. In difficult times, real friends make themselves known.

5. You will realize that some of your best friends do not know the real you, but only one part of you. In other words, they love you when you're happy, but not when you're sad.

6. There are those who would downplay your problems, because they are not life-threatening. You should run away from these people.

7. You will seek answers rather than the approval of others. This means that you are using your own judgment.

8. You will learn to take responsibility for your own life. You accept the consequences of your failures and do not blame others for your failures. You learn how to fight your own battles because not everyone is on your side.

9. It's hard, but you learn how to accept yourself. It's hard to be alone, and harder still to accept that it's your fault. You learn not to take things personally and to be strong when you are alone.

10. You will learn to deal with loneliness. You embrace your thoughts, your confusion, and your fears, and in the end, you learn to be fearless.

11. You learn that everyone in your life has a role to play, and that some roles are more important than others. You will learn that some roles are only temporary.

12. You will learn to be more cautious in future relationships. You are no longer so trusting, and you do not trust easily. You learn to set boundaries for those who do not have your best interest in mind.

13. You will learn that it is often better not to tell people everything about yourself, because you never know how or when they might use it against you.

14. You will realize that you can pick yourself up after a fall, and that you don't have to rely on anyone.

15. This is a difficult lesson, but also the most important one. You can survive alone, because some people just want to drag you down.

Why are so many people unable to stand behind their actions? Due to irresponsible behavior, we lose keys, money, jobs, housing, health, and even our lives. Children learn by being given chores, right?

Responsibility is a burden easily transferable to God, destiny, luck, or the next door neighbor. Responsibility was defined by the American journalist and satirical writer Ambrose Birrs in "Devil's Dictionary" printed back in 1911. A century has passed since he penned his definition, but nothing has changed. We still un-shoulder our responsibilities, pointing our finger at external elements that have broken our plans. So, we shift the blame for the delay to traffic jams, we did not continue our education because we had children, and the state is responsible because it does not provide the opportunity for us to move forward.

By definition, coming of age, is the moment when a child becomes an adult, ready to take on the responsibility for their actions. But, in reality, we act on that Voltaire's view that, no snowflake in the avalanche ever feels responsible, and we affirm Virginia Wolf's view that most people feel no responsibility for their actions.

Even the corporations have adopted the keyword of our age, insisting on social responsibility, but paradoxically, while we expect it from a colleague, our spouse, our friends, and our children, we find ourselves alone in giving it. Master psychologist and psychotherapist Danka Djukanovic says that if we belong to a group of overly responsible people, we may endanger our quality of life. But even so, we derive more benefit than harm.

Freud used to say that there are many people who do not want freedom, because they fear the responsibility. That describes you, the codependent—fearful of responsibility and its consequences. Djukanovic recalled the scenario we all experienced in childhood, our first broken toy. When asked by our parents, "Who did it?", we naively acknowledged our responsibility, and were punished.

You must become independent. That is an absolute priority because independence allows you to push back on your condition more forcefully.

This is akin to ripping off a band aid, and it will make your recovery much quicker.

10.1. What does independence mean for your condition?

Independence means taking care of yourself without constant support of other people. If you want to be independent, you need to hold your life in your hands and take care of it. Independence brings many responsibilities, but the freedom it brings is priceless.

If you fear independence—look at all its benefits:

10.2. A sense of freedom

Those who have never felt the freedom of independence can hardly imagine what that feeling is. You are completely dependent on yourself and you answer only to yourself. Independence allows you to make your own decisions, organize your time as you see fit, to do as you like, and to walk confidently down your chosen path.

10.3. More confidence

The very fact you are independent suggests progress. You have been able to give yourself the life you want through your hard work and dedication. The result is greater self-confidence as you witness your achievements mount.

The road to independence can be difficult, and scary. But with each step, your confidence builds. Each problem you solve increases your self-confidence.

10.4. Financial independence

Independence means be able to provide for your own needs, without the help of a parent, grandparent, or anyone else. Managing your own money, developing your financial management skills, and other skills you need to make your life as independent as possible, is truly rewarding.

Over time, you will realize that every obstacle you have overcome, and every effort you have put forth has been worth it. Now you can decide what matters to you, what you want to own—and you deserve that.

10.5. Better life decisions

When you are independent, all decisions are yours alone. Of course, you can seek advice, but the final decision is yours. Decision making is one of the more important, and perhaps most difficult thing in life, but over time you will learn how to analyze the problems, and make the right decision in the end.

10.6. Development of personality and character

Freedom, confidence, and financial independence are things that shape your persona, and your future. They bring your personality full circle, and you can make course corrections. Follow your every step, try to avoid mistakes, and make adjustments as you see fit. When you are independent and understand that your decisions are your own—you are ready to accept greater risks and bolder undertakings. This is how character is built. Opportunities are revealed, and so are the abilities that lie within you.

10.7. New value system

When you earn your own living, the value of money and time take on new meaning. You will gain an appreciation for your free time and those with whom you spend it. The more you value yourself and your life, the more you value the lives and decisions of the people in your circle. Going forward, your success will be viewed through a new lens, and your levels of motivation will increase. This brings positive change to your life, making it significantly better.

So get a firm grip, stand up, and face your problems.

But generally who else can help you in this process?

For those who experience substantial difficulties, such as inappropriate or destructive behavior, do harm to themselves etc., professional help (doctors, psychiatrists or psychologists) highly recommended.

Anyone with a mental condition has a better chance for recovery if they are motivated to change, volunteer for help, and have the support of loved ones. However, environmental distractions can sometimes harm them rather than help them. This typically arises from fear, or a failure to understand the nature of the problem. People in your environment may try to force you into treatment, or discourage treatment, either of which can cause you harm. So, first and foremost, listen to yourself.

10.8. About "mental illness"

Take depression for example. You hear about a person suffering from depression, you hear that they are *down*, others suggest "that she has to cope with herself", or that "only the mentally weak and incapacitated can suffer from depression". Sympathetic voices will say, "it is a shame to be depressed", or they have "surrendered." Still others will say," they are just acting out", or, they are "seeking attention", and similar nonsense. A person facing such prejudices will be "as depressed as depressed is possible ". Such comments compound their suffering, increases their isolation, diminishes trust, and may cause them to avoid seeking help or following prescribed therapies. This can end tragically. Yet another reason to rely on yourself.

10.9. Escape from reality

There is a palpable fear of being labeled, "people will think I'm crazy." If an individual cannot resolve their issues, it is time to contact an expert. If they allow problems, such as depression or anxiety, dominate their lives, the problem will only grow. The sooner you decide to seek help, the better.

I will remind you once again, because it is very important, that taking medication on your own, such as tranquilizers and sedatives, achieves nothing beyond short-term relief.

After only 3 weeks of drug use, addiction sets in, and over time, larger doses are required to achieve the same effect. These drugs artificially reduce suffering and as quickly as the drug is withdrawn, you are back to square one. Run from reality in this way, only makes the problem bigger. When used improperly, sedatives can speed up the process of dementia, and they can increase the risk of accidents in traffic and in the workplace. Don't try to escape reality. You can do this the right way.

10.10. What does the connection between the body and the psyche look like and how does the body respond to the signals that emotions send to it?

The brain stores our thoughts and shapes our beliefs, either under the influence of information from the outside world or, our internal world. Thoughts and beliefs are responsible for our emotional experience, that is to say, for how we will feel in a given situation. The body responds to our emotions, preparing for danger if we are afraid, or relaxing if we feel comfortable and safe. Every emotional response has a parallel response in our physical body. Through these bodily sensations, we can judge what emotions we are feeling. For example, when scared or anxious, adrenaline is released, blood vessels in the arms and legs expand as the body prepares for fight or flight, the stomach and intestines experience reduced blood supply, and the secretions of the protective envelope in the stomach are reduced...butterflies. The stomach cramps, resulting in that uncomfortable feeling of heaviness and tightness that we experience when we are anxious. The body, in this example, has established its priorities based on the fact that we are scared and in danger. If we are in danger, our muscles must be ready for action, and digesting food is completely irrelevant at that moment. Our body always respond in our best interests, but, and this is critical, our bodies respond on the basis of our emotional inputs. So, if those emotional inputs are flawed...God help us. Consequently, if our emotional response to the boss, the exam, and other everyday things is fear, then the body will respond accordingly. Stress levels go through the roof! Can you see the damage you can cause yourself if you delay solving your problem?

10.11. What helps you the most in your recovery is a rational view of the world around you

If we have an irrational view of what is happening in our lives, we will not have good outcomes. Every day we use terms with the potential to evoke depression, anxiety, and other unhealthy emotions, such as "I can't stand it!" Now that's a sentence that has weight. Suggesting something like that send our bodies a danger signal, engendering the appropriate. Here's an example, "I can't stand the boss criticizing me". Now that is inconsistent with the reality. If that were true, no one would leave his boss's office alive. It is indeed difficult, but bearable to deal with life's difficulties.

10.12. Look out for "magical cures"

Advertisements recommend products to boost self-confidence, implying that one has no self-confidence unless they use their product. Of course, we need self-confidence when we face challenges, but it isn't derived from a pill. If we lack self-confidence, a new challenge can make us anxious— we may even give up. However, if we approach this rationally, we will say, "Ok I have no experience in this situation, what should I do to gain it?" Then, as our experience increases, so does our self-confidence. Self-confidence parallels our experiences in specific life situations.

Be bold and consult with others as you move forward, but never lose sight of the fact that you are the master of your life. You have, metaphorically speaking, stepped into the ring. Now that you have your gloves on, don't give up. Fight like a lion. Do not hit below the belt, do not use the internet and do not self-medicate. Instead, read this book and consult your doctor. Eventually, believe it or not, you will be able to divert the river, and find that missing part of the clock.

CHAPTER THREE: USEFUL TOOLS

You've been through a lot so far, no doubt about it. But you are a tough and you are strong. Even though you are still missing the part needed to fix that watch, you are take huge strides forward. You have to that you are a victim in this story, and not the villain. I know that over the years you have developed feelings guilt. I know that you believe that you have tried your best to help others, and that you have pure intentions, but unfortunately, you have done the worst, for yourself and others. But don't despair, for every problem there is a solution.

Now you need relief. You understand what you have done. Your desperate desire to control others, thinking this would cure that sense of emptiness you have inside. I know you are suffering, but you have to be brave, you have to stand up, and build yourself up. You have to be emotionally born again. As I've told you before, there are multiple ways to control your emotions and facilitate your recovery.

In this chapter, I'll give you additional useful tools you can use when you experience a rush of emotions. There are ways to silence that voice in your head, even shut it off completely.

Breathing is essential for many emotional states. Believe it or not, breathing exercises might do the trick, and help you quiet that little voice in your head that urges you to intervene.

11.1. Benefits of breathing

There are 3 breathing exercises for calming the nervous system. They will reduce stress, induce relaxation, and restoring energy balance. You can suppress your control urges with these very effective tools.

You can do breathing exercises at any time. Since breathing can be controlled and regulated, it is a useful tool that we can use to a desired state of mind.

I recommend 3 breathing exercises, 1) stimulant breathing, 2) breathing exercise 4-7-8 (also called relaxing breath), and 3) exhalation counting.

11.2. Stimulant breathing

Stimulant breathing is a yogic breathing technique. Its purpose is to increase energy and alertness. Quickly inhale and exhale through the nose. Keep your mouth closed but relaxed. Your breaths and exhalations should be the same length but as short as possible. Don't hesitate, and breathe loudly. Try to do 3 breathe-in, breathe-out cycles per second. This will produce rapid movement of the diaphragm. Breathe normally after each cycle. To begin, do the exercise for a maximum of 15 seconds and increase that over time. The ultimate goal is to have a *stimulant breathing* exercise last for a full minute. Doing it properly will make you feel refreshed after exercise. While performing the exercise, you should feel a strain in the back of the neck, in the diaphragm, chest, and abdomen. The next time you want a cup of coffee, or feel your energy is low, do this breathing exercise.

11.3. Breathing Exercise 4-7-8 (Relaxing Breath)

Breathing 4-7-8 is extremely simple, although time-consuming, and can be done anywhere. Until you learn how to do it properly, exercise in a sitting position with your back straight. Place the tip of the tongue on the palate just behind the upper teeth and hold it there for the entire duration of the exercise. Exhale through the mouth so that air flows around the tongue. If this seems complicated, you can purse your lips slightly. As you exhale, make sure that you also produce sound at the same time. Then close your mouth and inhale softly through your nose, counting to four. Hold your breath for seven seconds and then exhale, only through your mouth for eight seconds. This is one cycle. After completing the first cycle, inhale again, and repeat the cycle 3 more times.

This breathing exercise helps calm the nervous system naturally. The effect of this breathing exercise will increase after prolonged practice. Do this exercise at least twice per day. During the first month, do a maximum of 4 cycles, and gradually increase to 8 cycles. You can do the exercise whenever you are stressed, have insomnia, or experience a rush of anger.

11.4. Exhalation counting

Exhalation counting is a Zen breathing exercise. It is simple exercise, but requires concentration. Sit in a comfortable position. Keep your spine straight and tilt your head slightly forward. Close your eyes, and take several deep breaths. After that, allow the breathing to flow naturally and try not to interfere. It is ideal to breathe quietly and slowly with deep sighs at different rhythms. To start the exercise, count the first exhalation as one. Count the second exhalation as 2 and continue until you reach 5. Then start a new breathing cycle from 1 to 5 (counting exhalations). Never work one cycle for more than five exhalations. It is advisable to do this for a total of 10 minutes.

11.5. Another very useful tool is relaxation techniques and they will be a great benefit for you.

Relaxation techniques for controlling anxiety and stress may be the best tool, so read this carefully. At the heart of any program to overcome anxiety, phobias or panic attacks is the ability to relax. Relaxing with TV, or a hot bath at the end of the day are examples of activities that can help us relax the mind. The type of relaxation required to reduce anxiety, is regular exercise that incorporates some form of deep relaxation. Deep relaxation refers to a specific physiological response that opposes your body's reaction to the stresses that you might experience in a panic attack or, a fight-or-flight scenario. This condition was first described by Herbert Benson in 1975 as a relaxing response.

11.6. What is a relaxing response?

It consists of a series of physiological changes, such as slowed breathing, lowered blood pressure, reduced muscle tension, slowed metabolic rate, reduced oxygen consumption, minimized analytical thinking, increased physiological resistance of the skin, and increased bio-electric alpha wave activity in the brain.

Practicing deep relaxation for 20 to 30 minutes a day can have positive effects over time. After a few weeks of daily deep relaxation, you will be more relaxed when engaged in other activities. Over the past 20 years, other beneficial effects of deep relaxation have been documented, such as relief from generalized anxiety. Many people have found that performing this exercise regularly reduces both the frequency and intensity of panic attacks.

11.7. *Prevention of stress accumulation*

Stress builds up over time. Getting daily physiological rest provides your body the opportunity to recover from the effects of stress. Even sleeping does not halt stress buildup unless you have allowed yourself to relax deeply when you are awake.

- Increased energy and productivity. (When stressed, you can work against yourself and become less effective.)
- Improved concentration and memory. Regularly engaging in deep relaxation exercises can increase your ability to concentrate and calm your mind.
- Reduced bouts of insomnia and fatigue. Learning to relax leads to deeper dream sleep.
- Prevents and/or reduces incidences of psychosomatic disorders such as high blood pressure, migraine, headache, asthma, ulcers, etc.
- Strengthens confidence and self-esteem. For many people, stress and self-criticism go hand-in-hand. When relaxed, you will feel better and function more efficiently.
- Increased ability to emote. Muscle tension is one of the principal factors that stop you from relating to your emotions.

11.8. How can you achieve a state of deep relaxation?

Some common methods are:

1. Abdominal breathing
2. Progressive muscle relaxation
3. Visualizing a calming scene
4. Meditation
5. Guided imagination
6. Autogenic training
7. Biological feedback from the body
8. Deprivation of the senses
9. Yoga
10. Calming music

So each time you experience symptoms, choose something from this list that best suits your needs. The point is that you sufficiently relax to overcome that river of emotions. Breathing exercises and relaxation techniques will help you to overcome your symptoms and better control your urges and emotions.

CHAPTER FOUR: SPECIFIC THERAPY SKILLS FOR TYPE CODEPENDENCY

First of all, codependent therapy must be very specific, because this condition is very specific. You are a unique individual whose condition requires significant attention, primarily from your loved ones.

Regardless of codependency type, what matters most is that you accept yourself. This is the most important step for you, as you move to improve your perception of life and the world around you. Going forward, you will see yourself as a completely different person. Your life will not be the one you know before, but that is essential for your recovery.

In every known type of codependency, the core cause and general symptoms are the same. Consequently, therapy will be mainly focused on developing your self-confidence and eliminating feelings of guilt.

Only when you have succeeded in boosting your self-confidence and erasing feelings of guilt, can you be certain that your therapy has been be fruitful. Yes, I know how you feel about yourself. I have already explained to you what the biggest problem with your condition is.

Your therapist will help you to understand the problem and understand the essence of the codependency. You have become your worst enemy. You have disregarded your life for the sake of others' lives, managing to lose yourself in the process. Look, this isn't me being judgmental—this is me telling you the truth. Only the truth can spare you from this condition.

You must be completely honest with your therapist. You must tell him everything that you've been through. Only in this way, can he develop the best treatment for you. Believe in yourself and just be honest. Only the truth can bring you to full recovery.

We already covered this, but I feel the need that you need to hear it again. You were always there to help others, and you put your life on hold for their sake. I understand that your intentions were good, and that you believed you were doing your best for yourself and for others. But unfortunately, this resulted in unfortunate consequences. People did not react to your good intentions with open arms, you were shocked that they resented you. I understand that you feel this way. However, you need to understand that you challenged *their* integrity, and devalued *their* self-worth. Because of that, they turned their backs on you.

12.1. What is integrity?

Integrity may be the most valuable thing that a person has. Integrity is the boundary that separates independent people from the rest. People do all that they can to protect themselves and their integrity. You, on the other hand, don't have this crucial quality. You need to learn how to protect your integrity and you need integrity to make your life better and create a new you.

12.2. What you need to know

With integrity, self-confidence will improve drastically. So there are things to which you must say *no*. Forget about other people's needs, and recognize that they may exploit your willingness to make compromises. Remember that every time you make a compromise, that you don't really want to make, a small piece of your personality will vanish.

Always remember that you are a good person and will always be a good person. That doesn't mean that you have to be everyone's savior. The world is not your problem. Rather than trying to care for the world and everyone in it, you must realize that you can't save everyone Instead of trying to care for everyone, start to think about yourself, your life, and your personal needs. It is not in our power to change the world. That is macro-level and unattainable. So, focus your actions on the micro- level.

12.3. The micro-level

I will define micro-level as a universe of one—you. Your life and your environment. You must begin to focus on yourself. Each day, ask yourself this question, "What can I do today to make my life better?"

12.4. Learn how to be happy

You always feel that senseless guilt for everything you do. Is that correct? Can you recall the last time you had a good time and didn't feel guilty about it?

You can't, because you are overwhelmed with guilt. Feelings of guilt are your worst enemy. Ask yourself, why? Why are you guilty? If you analyze it carefully you can arrive at only one logical conclusion. There is no reason for that feeling. That feeling was caused by a traumatic event, and it denies your happiness.

12.5. The message

In addition to your therapy, you must understand everything that I written here. No, you are not guilty of anything, and no, you are not a superhero—so, stop with the obsessive need to control. You will never win a single battle as long as you continue to compensate for helping others. For once, focus on yourself and on your life.

CHAPTER FIVE: HELPFUL STRATEGIES WHEN A LOVED ONE HAS CODEPENDENCY

This chapter is not intended for persons suffering from this condition. This chapter is for those of you who are living with a person that suffers from this condition and who you want to help. You love this person or you wouldn't read this book. By now, you've had the opportunity to become familiar with all aspects of the codependency condition.

What is important now, is to help your loved one. Let's be clear from the start. I understand that living with a person who suffers from this condition is not easy, but you read this book because you want to help them. So, here are some useful strategies to help your loved one.

13.1. What is essential?

When a person manifests one of the psychic symptoms, the initial reaction of their loved ones is denial. Denial is an unhelpful escape from a painful reality. First reactions also depend on cultural norms and prevailing attitudes within the family. In some families, mental health care is an integral part of caring for oneself and loved ones, while in others the topic is not discussed, because mental health problems are equated with weakness. Families who normalize the existence of mental health problems will be quicker to accept the existence of the problem and seek professional help. In other families, the period between acknowledging the problem and seeking professional help is usually longer. The person who has the problem copes as best they can, and fears that they will be labeled as weak, and inadequate. Support, understanding, caring, and love provides hope that recovery is possible. In the absence of the above, recovery is significantly impeded.

13.2. What are the steps in supporting a loved one?

Sometimes a codependent person will share the story of the difficulties they are experiencing. Although this can make dealing with the situation easier, frequently, family members respond by denying the severity of the problem. Unlike the aforementioned denials, denying the severity of the symptoms, sends the message, "You can do this, it is not so terrible, you have succeeded so much, look how it has worked...." Frankly, such conversations are not helpful, making the codependent feel less competent, and the problem confronting them less solvable. The truth is, no one, not even a professional, can feel what the person with anxiety, depression, obsessive thoughts, anorexia, and especially codependency, feels They can still help, though. Not only because of the knowledge they have, but also by listening carefully to what the person is saying about the problem. So, if one is exposed to a problem, the first step is to hear it, hear it in the full scope of its intensity. It would more appropriate to say, "I don't understand, because I've never felt something like that, but it seems like a very difficult experience for you."

Sometimes the responsibility of recognizing the symptoms falls on loved ones. The situation is a little more complex then, but they must always try to understand that the codependent may be ashamed, and afraid to share what is bothering them. Many mental illnesses alter the sufferer's perception of reality and prevent them from recognizing that they are in trouble. A timely response can significantly shorten the course of recovery. Loved ones have a moral responsibility to seek professional help for the codependent, despite their resistance and denial. Approaching the codependent by expressing feelings of concern regarding perceived symptoms or behaviors, offering hope that recovery is possible, giving clear information that the person is not alone, that they are loved and accepted is encouraged. Tolerating certain behaviors, such as drinking, gambling, eating disorders, matters of personal hygiene, and failing to participate in daily activities must not be ignored. That would be tantamount to fostering disease. Family members must understand that making good decisions are crucial in reversing the development of the disease.

13.3. *The second step is to seek professional help*

Loved ones can provide support by encouraging the codependent to schedule a medical examination or talk to a psychotherapist. If professional assistance is in progress, further assistance, such as scheduling medications, keeping appointments, arranging follow-ups, and so forth, are very helpful.

13.4. *The third step is to provide ongoing support*

Most loved ones want to provide support but don't know how. Seeking answers from both the expert and the codependent gives you the clearest guidance. There is no need for anyone to be alone and in the darkness. There is always a path. Being a good listener and asking questions regarding the codependent's thoughts and feelings, combined with an open acknowledgement of the codependent's significant role they play in everyone's life, and that codependency is the problem, not the codependent. They are still a good person, with many positive qualities and unrealized potential. Even when the codependent offers no resistance to professional help, the loyalty and support of loved ones plays an irreplaceable and invaluable role. Codependent should recognize that not only they but also their loved ones, are going through difficult times. The experience of speaking with an expert, in the presence of the codependent, can make things easier for everyone. For the codependent, support means having someone who understands what is being discussed, and what is happening to them. And, knowing that an expert is providing loved ones with neutral information that dispels misconceptions and prejudices. Those with anxiety or depressive disorders, regardless of the support they receive (joint visits with physicians/psychotherapists), are occasionally misunderstood, labeled as cowards, lazy, and irresponsible. As noted above, each of these messages is a stumbling block to recovery.

13.5. Control

The fourth step, which occurs after becoming acquainted with the problem in detail, is the control of relapse (recurrence of symptoms). Loved ones, already familiar with the problem and the symptoms, will recognize them if they reappear. Although relapse is discouraging, it is important not to give up, and seek professional help as soon as possible. Taking that first step towards treatment is always difficult, be it parents or children, husband or wife, or friend. We must understand that psychological difficulties are not a measure of a person's strengths or weaknesses. The person is still the same person, except now, they have a problem. The codependent will soon come to stabilization and/or recovery, with love, support, care, and the freedom to communicate their problems.

So the basic message is simple. Be as supportive as possible, and learn to cope with this condition. Take no actions that may activate the triggers you've read about here, and convince your loved one to begin therapy. Do these things, and have unlimited patience with your loved one.

Remember that your loved one is a victim. and it is your loved one that suffers the most. Now, I know that you might not believe that, but unfortunately, that is the truth. The codependent person is difficult for you in many respects, but you still love that person. The codependent is dealing with enormous levels of guilt, shame, and depression. The effect of a traumatic experience looms large inside that person. You can salvage your loved one only if you are willing to overcome your own ego and dismiss the past. Be supportive, and be compassionate. Do not be judgmental, because that will only backfire. If you can't accept your loved one and forgive their transgressions, you will lose that person forever. Don't make that mistake. Suppress any anger and resentment you may feel, and do the right thing. If you can do that, the person you love will heal, and both of you will have a whole new life.

CHAPTER SIX: WHAT PEOPLE AROUND YOU NEED TO KNOW IN ORDER TO HELP YOU?

What your family needs to know to help you

We'll talk about *you* again. This is also very important. Until now, you didn't know why your watch wasn't ticking. Now you know a great deal. Before reading this book, all you knew, was that something wasn't right.

Now you know what it is. It's time to be brave. Time to realize that even though you are alone in this fight, you are not without the support of others. When I told you this was your fight I meant you were the one who has to stake the initiative and demonstrate the will to overcome this condition. It means that, in a manner of speaking, you must defeat yourself—do you understand?

As for the people around you, it's best to be open and honest, about your problem. Just as you have to be honest with yourself, so you have to be honest with others. We've already said that running away from reality is a dead end. It's the same with running away from the truth. Honesty is the best medicine. There is a saying that, "the worst truth is always better than the most beautiful lie". It's time to explain your condition to your family. They, just like you, live in the dark when it comes to your behavior. They tried to understand you but couldn't. Now it's time to explain to them what is going on, so that your family can finally know what is important regarding your condition.

14.1. Why family is the only important social network

The famous meme that all happy families look like each other has already been written by one of the greatest writers, but a hundred years later, it remains the absolute truth.

They say that everything comes from family. Family can be your greatest strength, as well as your greatest weakness. Certainly, there are times when our loved ones drive us crazy, but when times are tough, you always come home.

Many families have been together for decades. What makes a family the happiest is the absence of conflict, closeness, mutual understanding, respect, shared activities, and the support of loved ones. When a family has all of that, then difficulties become nothing more than small bumps in the road.

Most modern families have a strong social network, which includes immediate and extended family members as well as friends. Most believe that they can rely on this social network when they need support. This is consistent with large international studies, which indicate that families in transitional societies are vital, and that the family network provides emotional, social and economic assistance to its members. Strangely, in developed Scandinavian countries with high levels of wealth, material goods and social support from the state, there has been a decline in close family relationships. Research indicates that strong social networks which are closely related to close relationships and emotional exchange, are stronger in transitional societies.

Psychological research into happiness has shown that there are three different types of happiness, 1) happiness in a *Hollywood sense* that involves relaxation, smiling and satisfying desires, 2) happiness related to engaging in activities that have a deeper meaning for the person, and 3) happiness originating from the feeling that our life has a purpose and that we are connected to something bigger than ourselves.

So, it is the family that understands you best. The support you need for your recovery will be found in your family, but only if you are honest with yourself and with your family. If they choose not to support you, so be it. That will only make you stronger and you will manage to overcome your condition regardless.

What your partner needs to know to help you

Your partner, your soul mate, needs to know everything there is to know. You must be completely honest with your loved one and you must tell them everything there is to know.

I want to be very clear about this. If you love someone and you learn something that you didn't know before—you must tell your partner everything. You need to be responsible and completely honest. You must bare yourself to the bone.

While positive vibes and wide smiles create the need to be a part of your loved one's life and share all the joy with them, your problems, negative thoughts and failures can cause you to close the door to your loved one. Fighting to communicate with someone who seeks isolation is difficult, but love is the weapon that can help you tear down those walls. There are several ways to initiate a conversation. Love and tenderness can motivate you to open up to your partner, and begin a discussion regarding your problems and insecurities. This makes it easier for your partner to understand what you did and why you did it. The same applies to you. If you want support you have to be honest.

The moment we first face the problem, we need some space to isolate ourselves, think about everything, and work out how to solve the problem. In such moments that the partner needs to be given some time to process everything.

When we are in emotional distress, we may not be aware of our inaccessibility, so try to let them know that there is no need for walls. You are in this together.

14.2. Give them understanding

Even if they push you away in difficult times, remember, he wasn't aware of your problem. Give them the understanding and support they need, they can help you to overcome the crisis and accept your issues. When you feel their support and understanding, you will begin open up to them.

In addition to love and trust, communication is one of the most important factors for a successful and healthy relationship. If there isn't good communication between the partners, there can be trust issues, stress, misunderstandings, and unnecessary quarrels. For all that, be honest. This is the only way for your partner to understand you and for you to overcome this problem together.

-What your friend needs to know to help you

Your friend can be a very important person regarding your condition. If you have someone in your life, whom you've known for a very long time, and you are extremely close, they may be able to help you the most. The same openness and honesty applies to such a friend.

14.3. Why is friendship important

It's hard to imagine a life without friends; they are an integral part of our lives. They make us happy, and they cheer us up when we are down. It is extremely difficult to find a true friend, and when one has one or two friends in their life, it can be said that this person is truly blessed. It's clear why friendship is important. A true friend is hard to find.

Fake friendships are an everyday occurrence. We have countless people that come in and out of our lives, but only the right ones survive. Once you have experienced disappointment, it can be difficult to take another gamble on friendship, especially when it comes to trust, honesty, and closeness. But sometimes friendship is the most beautiful and deepest of all relationships. Friendship is not easy, it requires a mutual give and take.

It is not enough that others are with you. You must also be with them. That means being there for the good times and the bad times. In today's world, this is true wealth, and a true friend has immeasurable value. True friendship means a great deal of responsibility. You must be responsible and acknowledge your obligation to your friends. Friendship is, by no means, a matter of self-interest. If you hang out with someone for the benefits, then it is not a true friendship.

True friendship means mutual respect. Respect is important in every relationship, and where there is no respect, there is no relationship. Love your friend in spite of their faults and accept them for who they are. Trusting someone is rare these days, and when you gain that trust, you gain a fortune. True friends are always there for you, and would not betray you under any circumstances. Open up to your friend, trust him, and tell him your problems. An open heart and trust contribute to understanding. For a true friend, you open your heart, and give them a special place in it, and they, in turn, will give you their love.

Friendship means forgiveness, and asking for forgiveness. Be big enough to ask for forgiveness when you are wrong. A true friend will forgive you, but do not show them disrespect by repeating the same mistakes. Life is not easy, it brings both good and bad, ups and downs, but when you have the support of a true friend, you will push through. The hand of friendship is the most wonderful thing a person can achieve in life. True friendships are rare. So, if you are fortunate to have one, cherish it.

A good friend is worth a thousand acquaintances. If you have a good friend tell him everything and know he will be with you. Openness means a lot.

14.4. Why are good friends so important?

Many studies have looked at the benefits of friendship, and have confirmed what you have already assumed. The better the friendships you have, the happier you are. Therefore, it is good for your happiness to be someone's best friend, and have a group of good friends who support you. Sometimes it's hard to determine what makes a good friend.

14.5. Good friend signs

Friends will come in and out of your life, but more important than how long a friendship lasts, is that your friend loves you for who you are. You can recognize a good friend by his deeds, large and small, which show you that they care.

A good friend is:

- Someone who will support you, no matter what
- Someone you can trust and who doesn't condemn you
- Someone who will not let you down or intentionally hurt you
- Someone kind and respectful to you
- Someone who loves you because they have made that choice, not because they need it
- Someone you enjoy being with
- Someone who shows loyalty
- Someone trustworthy and who tells the truth, even when it is difficult
- Someone who laughs with you
- Someone who is with you when you have a problem
- Someone who makes you laugh
- Someone who listens to you
- Someone who will cry with you too.

14.6. Friendship and why them

The importance of friendship is best understood if you concentrate for a moment and try to think of at least one person who has never had a friend, and probably never will. Try it. It's not possible, is it? Even humanity's biggest monsters have friends. So the phenomenon of friendship is a universal and therefore, deserves special attention.

14.7. Friendship and some psychological interpretations

Friendly relationships, even deep ones, can develop as early as childhood. As an individual's personality develops, these relationships gain new qualities. People set new tasks both to themselves and to others. Peers, and especially close friends, have a great influence on the individual, especially during adolescence. During this period, when young people struggle for psychological independence from their parents, friends exert a substantial influence in forming one's self-image, attitudes, aspirations. Friends can motivate an individual to adopt different behaviors, and friends have an active role in the development of one's identity.

In psychology, one aspect of self-image is called the social self. It encompasses perceptions of interpersonal relationships, their moral attitudes, and vocational/educational goals. If these social relationships in a person's life are disturbed, they have a very negative effect on the self-image, not the mental health in general, but the young person's stability.

Friends play a big role during the period in which the young person defies the authority of their parents, and begin to choose goals for themselves. For a young person, having a mature and stable friend means having direction. The kind of direction needed to find yourself in the newly discovered world of social relationships outside the family. The influence of peers and friends is third in order (after family and teacher) in the process of professional orientation and choice of future occupation. In the mature period, the situation is a little different.

Abraham Maslov, one of the representatives of the humanistic direction in psychology, says everyone strives toward his ultimate goal, which is self-actualization. In simple words, the self-actualized personality is the one who has realized the maximum of all their real potentials, achieved the highest they could, and they are finally satisfied. This motive is at the top of the scale of human motives. One of the characteristics of a self-actualized personality is that they establish a small number of deep relationships with people, and they have the occasional need for solitude. As adults we have a built-in social relations system that seeks to maintain our satisfaction.

In daily life, the mature personality increasingly relies on himself and his personal experience, welcoming friends and taking time for them in times of crisis or periods of joy. As we age, one develops more realistic expectations and more mature approaches to connecting with people. That's how it should be. Jung also spoke about friendship, saying, "If you're lonely, it's because you chose it".

So don't reject a friend, and don't "keep him in the dark" about you and your condition. A good friend is a treasure. You will find many shells, but if you are very lucky, you will find a pearl or two. So, you need to open yourself to your friend and apologize for everything that your condition may have caused between two of you, and then you will have the support you need.

-What your children need to know to help you

If you have children the best thing you can do for them is just to hug them and say to them "I love you, everything will be better from now on".

If your children are small, you can't explain to them that you have a condition, and that because of your condition you behaved badly. They are small, and just starting to learn about the world around them. You don't need to burden them with the story of your condition. They probably won't understand it. There's a good chance that many adults won't understand, let alone children.

Regarding your children, you must be able to suppress everything that you carry inside. You need to open your heart and... just love them. Love them beyond any measure and spend as much of your time as can with them. Don't refuse them anything. If you are not on the best of terms, do everything in your power to restore the relationship with your children. Remember, this is a new you, a responsible you, and your children deserve a good childhood.

Your condition is curable, and one day soon, you will be much better, both for yourself and for your children. I will tell you a story. I knew a man who suffered from schizophrenia. When doctors told him that he was suffering from this horrible mental illness, he told me, but he never allowed his children know about his illness. He managed to fight his mental illness (with severe medication) successfully for three years, and he gave his children three more years of pure happiness. When he felt that he could no longer suppress his illness, he voluntarily entered a mental institution for fear that he might hurt them. That was a truly brave man. I told you this story because I wanted you to understand what parental sacrifice means.

Remember to put your children in first place, always and forever. You will eventually get better, and when they are old enough, you will tell them about your condition and how you fought it and beat it.

CHAPTER SEVEN: START YOUR HEALING PROCESS AND LEARN HOW TO LOVE AGAIN

Everything you have learned so far is essential for you to start your healing process and to learn how to love again. It is not easy to accept yourself and all your mistakes. However, if you succeed in doing this, you will remove your concerns from your life, and at the same time, you will no longer be devastated should someone criticize you.

The easier it is to accept yourself, the easier it is to accept others. Treat yourself the way you want others to treat you, rely on yourself in the same way you want to rely on your partner. When you succeed in this, you will have something to give to others.

It seems to me that basic wisdom says, if you do not love yourself, you cannot love others. When you do not love yourself, you cannot understand yourself, and become prone to self-criticism. Self-criticizing for fearing loneliness, entering relationships for the wrong reasons, or being mired in in the wrong relationship.

When you do not love yourself, you view the love relationship as the beginning and the end of everything, especially your happiness, and even life itself. So, you are prepared to sacrifice yourself and your needs for others. When you lose a loved one, especially if you feel rejected, you lose yourself too, unless you love yourself.

15.1. Does every criticism and remark touch your heart?

If this is happening, then you are not very happy with yourself. Change some habits and change the way you think.

15.2. Tips for making it easier for you to accept yourself

Remember one or two minor mistakes you know you've made. Tell yourself that in ten years they will be gone, so, it doesn't matter if they exist now. You may not yet understand why you have made certain mistakes, but over time, you will understand.

At least once per day, remember that all people have good and bad characteristics. Be patient with yourself. You haven't stopped learning — we learn throughout our lives. If you believe in a higher power, then convince yourself that the higher power loves you as you are. Your parents love you in the same way. Learn to pamper yourself without spending a lot, and show yourself that you love yourself. Think of the characteristics that you do not like and cannot change. Is there something in these characteristics that you could love? Think of someone you love. Do you love him despite his flaws?

15.3. Practice Receiving Love

If you want to truly love, you must receive love and be aware that you deserve it. Accept the love given by your loved ones, their good deeds, kind words, compliments, and gifts. Practice saying "I love you" to yourself, love yourself unconditionally and such love will fill your heart.

15.4. Practice saying "no"

Don't feel guilty about rejecting someone or not being in the mood to do something that others are asking you to do. Do only what your heart desires, and do nothing to please others.

15.5. Do what you love

If you can find something you love to do and begin spending time doing it, you will find love, joy, and happiness in your heart.

15.6. Treat yourself as your best friend

Leave the past behind and be present for every new day. Forgive yourself for all your mistakes, regrets, and omissions. It's time to move forward.

15.7. Nurture yourself

Find time for yourself. Nurture yourself physically, emotionally, mentally and spiritually. Do that which gives you a sense of peace, joy, and love. Take a walk, play sports, exercise, dance, eat healthy and sleep.

15.8. Feel good with yourself

Look in the mirror, smile and say to yourself "I love myself, I'm worthy of love". Listen to your favorite music, read books, play with pets, be proud of your accomplishments, write a diary of your life dreams and goals.

15.9. Don't compare yourself with others

Every human being is unique, and everyone has a different talent. Comparing yourself with others evokes negative emotions, such as impaired self-esteem, depression, envy, and jealousy. Focus on your inner strength, get to know yourself, and discover the gifts you have.

15.10. You don't have to be perfect

Stop criticizing yourself for not being perfect. Strive to give your best, and if you do not achieve perfection, accept that it does not mean defeat.

15.11. And something else

When you reach that point when you can say that you accept yourself, many things will change. Your world view will change, you will become more tolerant of others, and it will be easier to accept criticism on your account. Remarks will not affect you, because deep down you know you love yourself.

15.12. Now is the time

It's time to believe in yourself again. It's time to move on with your life. It is time to surrender to your past self. It's time to believe in good. It's time to leave behind all the painful memories. It's time to focus on what matters most—your happiness.

Now begins a new chapter for you. The story has not yet ended. It is time to embrace all that has happened, to learn the lessons, and to continue your journey. It is time to free your heart from all the pain you feel and learn to love yourself and your life again.

Happiness is not only external but also internal—and this internal happiness is special, because it is purer and more honest than any other kind of happiness. And you can only achieve it when you learn to appreciate yourself for who you are. When you choose not to be so rude to yourself, and when you realize that you are wrong, and still take a step forward because you do not want to be caught in the grip of the past. It is time for you to continue on your path.

15.13. Always remember to love yourself

After all, loving yourself is the most important thing you can do in this life. Through life, you experience many things. Beautiful moments and moments that are less than beautiful. You will know not only the good, but also the evil, not only happiness, but also sadness. So I will ask you to be gentle with yourself, be patient…because what you have inside you is a relationship that will last forever. Understand that you have no control over anything that happens in your life. Not over feelings, and not over people.

15.14. At the end

Happiness is not the absence of problems, but the ability to face them. Just imagine what wonderful things your mind could achieve if it weren't so focused on dealing with problems. Always look at what you have, instead of what you have lost. It doesn't matter what life has taken from you, but what you will do with what you have left.

15.15. Here are some reminders to help you get motivated when you need it.

1. Pain is part of the growth process

Sometimes life closes the door because we need to move forward. And that is a good thing, because we often do not want to make a move until circumstances force us. When times are tough, remember that no pain comes without purpose. Step away from what hurts, but never forget what it taught you. Just because you lost some fights does not mean you are unsuccessful. Every great success requires some kind of good fight to get there. Good things take time. Be patient and positive. Everything will work out, if not immediately, then when the time comes.

There are two types of pain—one that hurts you, and one that changes you. Don't resist them because they both teach you how to grow.

2. Everything in life is transient

Every time it rains, it stops. Every time you are hurt, you heal. After darkness comes the light. Each morning reminds us, but we often forget and believe that the night will last forever. It won't. Nothing in this world lasts forever. So if all is well now, enjoy it. It won't last forever. If things go downhill, don't worry because that won't last forever either. Just because life isn't easy right now doesn't mean you can't laugh. Just because something is bothering you doesn't mean you can't smile. Each moment offers you a new beginning and a new end. Every second, you get a second chance. You just have to accept things and do the best you can.

3. Concerns and lamentations change nothing

Those who mourn the most achieve the least. It is always better to try to do something big and fail, than to not try at all. All is not finished if you have lost, it is finished when you do nothing. If you believe in something, keep trying. Don't let the shadows of the past darken the passage to your future. If we mourn today because of yesterday, it will not make tomorrow better. Instead, do something. Make what you have learned enhance your life. Make a change and look no further. And no matter what happens, in the long run, that true happiness only begins when you stop complaining about your problems, and learn to be grateful for any problems you do not have.

4. Your scars are symbols of your strength

Don't be ashamed of the scars life has left upon you. The scar means that the pain has stopped and the wound is healed. Scarring means you overcame the pain, learned the lesson, got stronger, and moved on. A scar is a triumphant tattoo—be proud of it. Don't let scars hold you hostage. Don't let them make you live your life in fear. You can't make them go away, but you can change the way you look at them. Start seeing the scars as signs of your strength, it doesn't hurt anymore.

5. Every fight is a step forward

In life, patience is not a matter of waiting; it is the ability to maintain a good attitude while we work hard on our dreams, knowing that the work is worth it. So, if you decide to give it a try, invest the time, and go all the way. Otherwise, it doesn't even make sense to start. This may mean that you will lose stability and comfort for a time, and occasionally your mind. This may mean that you will not eat anything, and sleep where you can, for a while. It can mean that you stretch your comfort zone so much that you feel a constant tingling. This can mean sacrificing relationships, and everything you've come to know. This may mean that someone will make fun of you, or that you will be lonely for a while. Loneliness can be a gift that makes things possible. It gives you the space you need. Everything is a test of your determination.

And if you want something, you will what is necessary, regardless of failures, rejections, and expectations. At every turn, you will feel better than you can imagine. You will understand that combat is not the way to go, it is the way itself. And it pays off. Therefore, if you are going to try, go all the way. There is no better feeling in the world... there is no better feeling than knowing what it means to be alive.

6.   Other people's negativity is not your problem

Be positive when negativity surrounds you. Smile when others want to put you down. It's an easy way to keep your enthusiasm and focus in check. When people treat you poorly, continue to be who you are. Don't let resentment change you. Don't take things personally, even when they seem be personal. People rarely do things for you. They do it for themselves. Above all else, never change yourself to impress someone who says you are not good enough. Change because it makes you a better person, and because it leads you to a better future. People will gossip no matter what you do, and how well you do it. So take care of yourself, no regard to what others think. If you believe in something, don't be afraid to fight for it. Great power comes from overcoming that which others believe is impossible to overcome. You only live this life once. Use it wisely. Do what makes you happy, makes you a better person and brings a smile to your face.

7.   Ultimately, it will be as it should be

Real power comes when you have so many reasons to cry, but instead, choose to smile. There is some blessing in every struggle we face, but to see it, it is necessary to have an open heart and mind. You can't force things to happen. You can just go crazy trying. At some point, all you have to do is let what happens, happen. Loving your life means trusting your intuition, taking risks, losing and finding happiness, cherishing memories and learning from experiences. It is a long-distance journey. Stop worrying and doubting yourself every step of the way. Live consciously, in the moment, and enjoy what life brings you. You may not end up where you planned to go, but you will end up where you need to be.

8.   The best you can do is move on

Do not be afraid to stand on your own two feet again. Don't be afraid to love again. Don't let the cracks in your heart turn into scars. Find the courage to be different, but still beautiful. Find in your heart the desire to make others laugh. Remember that you don't need a lot of people in your life, just a few wonderful ones. Be strong when things go downhill. Remember that the universe always does what is right. Recognize when you are wrong, and learn from it. Always look back and see how you've grown, and be proud of yourself for that. Don't change for the sake of others.

What more can I say to you? It's time to put everything that has happened behind you. End that chapter of your life with a calm soul and a broad smile. Remember to accept the next chapter. Get on with your life.

PART 3

CHAPTER ONE: LIVING WITH A CODEPENDENT PERSON

This chapter is for all of you who are living the life of a codependent person. If you've reading this far, you know the truth, both about the codependent person and about yourself. I believe that deep down, you already know how to live with a codependent person, and how you view that connection now. Having read this book thus far, you could only conclude, that you are a victim as much as your codependent partner is a victim and you understand that it is not their fault that things went bad. It's up to you to decide how to move forward. You can support a codependent person, which is certainly important, but maybe this kind of relationship has become too much for you.

My recommendation for you is, that knowing the truth, you will be supportive to your codependent partner. Remember, behind all your disagreements, is the person suffering from this condition.

For some, love relationships and partnerships are a source of energy for coping with life's challenges, while for others, it is an energy field that sucks the life from you causes many problems.

One of the most common problems in such relationships is the dependence. Some emerging clients recognize that they are addicted, and want to overcome this challenge, but there are large numbers of people who are not aware of their addiction, but only recognize the many symptoms that have arisen from it.

16.1. Five basic signs of addiction

1. Although your mind tells you that the relationship is hurting you, and that you cannot expect any improvement, you take no concrete steps to end it.

2. You give yourself irrational reasons for maintaining the connection that are an insufficient counter to the negative aspects of the relationship.
3. When you think about breaking up, you feel fear, even horror, so hold on to it even more.
4. When you take steps to break up, you suffer from acute symptoms of separation anxiety, which includes physical and emotional pain, only alleviated by reestablishing the relationship.
5. When the relationship is ended (or so you think), you feel lost, lonely, and empty...an abandoned person, but simultaneously, you feel a sense of liberation.

If most of these signs are present, you can be reasonably sure that you are in a relationship in which the elements of addiction have taken control of your ability to manage your life. The first step in resolving this addiction is to acknowledge that it exists, after which you need to learn how it works. The next steps are focused on empowering you as an individual, leading you to a degree of freedom, and then you can decide whether the relationship should be improved, accepted or ended.

And lastly, the message I always emphasize that goes beyond being dependent on a partner. Let your relationship with a codependent person be a choice, not a commitment.

I have an opinion that I feel the need to share with you.

You have to look at all of this through the lens of pure logic. If you have lived with a codependent person all this time, and you were unaware of this condition, why would you leave the relationship now that you know the truth? That just isn't logical to me. You have a unique opportunity now. You can help a codependent person now. You have all the necessary tools to help that person in this book. My advice to you is simple—don't give up.

16.2. How to Save a Relationship before you break up

- Don't give up on love

If you are not happy about the relationship, and you are facing problems, do not give up and end a relationship that used to be great. Keep in mind that many couples are in crisis, but that doesn't mean you have to break up.

Here are some things you can try to help save the bond that is about to break.

- Communicate as a team

One of the worst things to do is to break up without discussing it openly. Remember that. "You don't want to permanently hurt someone's feelings, and at the same time, you have to talk openly and honestly about why the relationship doesn't work," says relationship expert Rory Sasun. Be kind, and talk sensitively, so that the partner responds in kind, and feels safe to speak honestly and openly.

- Say yes

If things don't work out or you get into a routine, try putting some excitement into the mix. "It may seem counterproductive for you to say yes, when your relationship is on the verge of breaking up. The idea is to give yourself a whole lot of room to save the relationship," says relationship expert Marla Martenson. Try to rediscover the excitement and adventure of the relationship, be ready to help, and try to smooth things out where they don't work.

- Get rid of bad memories

Make a pact to start over, and to explore opportunities for a happy future. "One of my favorite techniques is to practice deliberately forgetting all the bad shared memories a couple has, and only remembering good things," says Martenson.

Usually, when the relationship is on the verge of breaking up, there is a lot of resentment and negative thoughts among the partners. By practicing this, so-called selective amnesia, you can get rid of the ugly past and enjoy the present.

- Be patient after a big conversation

If you had the big conversation where you talked about your feelings, don't expect things to change overnight. Be patient, and if things don't improve, then think again about your relationship. After talking to your partner about what's not working and why you're not happy, you should be patient and give your partner a chance to make some changes.

- Set specific goals

Communication is important, but it will be more effective if you set specific goals and an action plan. Instead of talking and then moving on, set goals for your relationship. This may include weekly meetings to converse, network, go out together. Treat each other as you did at the beginning of a relationship

- Try to treat your partner as if the relationship was just starting.

That means making your partner the priority, thinking about them constantly, and thinking of ways to make them happy.

- Do something different and spontaneous

Do you remember the 2:00 AM walks and late night talks in the early phase of your relationship? A time when it seemed that nothing else in the world mattered? Try to recreate those things that made you so happy in the beginning. Change your routine! Do something new with your partner, whether it's running or playing tennis.

- Make your partner happy

How does a partner express their love and affection— sweet words, gifts, time together, physical touch? Think about it, and do just that, to revive your love and save your relationship.

- Focus on your partner's positive traits

Are you constantly telling your partner how they should change? Do you focus on traits that annoy you? Stop it! Try to remember everything positive about your partner. List the reasons you love them and focus that! Even when they do something that annoys you, counter it by remembering something about them that you love.

- Work on yourself too

Sometimes your personality is the cause for stagnation and negativity in the relationship. When we become the best version of ourselves, then we create the best possible relationship. When I see people stuck in unhealthy relationships, it's often because they don't stop to look at how they can improve themselves. Work on yourself, then!

- Spend some time separately

Take a short break, and find some alone time. That will provide you time to think things through, and who knows, maybe that space that you give yourself will reawaken the love and desire you experienced in the early days of the relationship.

- Make small gestures that show you care

Simply put a smile on your partner's face. Love is a word. You have to understand that actions speak louder than words. Make it your daily habit to do one thing that makes your partner happy. See how that changes how you feel about your partner, and how they feel about you.

Connections can be difficult, but with a little effort, they can succeed. Healthy relationships take time, and breaking up is not always the answer.

Make sure you keep your relationship, and simultaneously help the person you love. It's always easier to turn your back and run, but you know the truth now. You must make the effort to help your codependent partner.

CHAPTER TWO: WHY DID
THEY CHOOSE YOU?

With regard to this specific question, the psychiatric community hasn't provided definitive and concrete answers. When it comes to love and codependency there are only speculations. Why and how a codependent personality chooses their partner is largely unknown. Scholars have provided some theories, but provable reasons are unclear. So, if you think that there is something specific in your personality that attracted a codependent person to you, you need to stop doing that. The only answer given, that we only partially accept, is that codependent persons are attracted to strong personality types. Even that has not been proven.

The question is a relative one, but when it comes to love, it is not a question for the brain but for the heart. All that researchers can tell us, is that codependent people seem to exhibit a pattern in choosing their partners.

17.1. The choice is never random

The question should be; why don't codependents choose partners with whom they can form harmonious love relationships? Instead, codependents choose to enter into unstable and unsatisfactory love relationships. The reason for this is that codependent persons are usually inconsistent people. They are a jumble of different personality traits. Because of this, they function in conflicting ways. While on one level they make choices based upon reason, on another level, they make choices based upon chemistry, that is, based upon subconscious processes. These subconscious processes, which often come from the adult's *inner child*, create strong emotions that often overcome the rational method.

Either way, the choice of a partner never random, there is always a method. When the methodology is revealed, we learn that it speaks more about the person who chooses than about the person who is selected.

A codependent that consistently chooses a partner who is cold, emotionally distant, and unavailable, makes that choice because their *inner child* needs a challenge. The codependent is driven by the subconscious logic that suggests that by attracting this type of person, they will affirm their worth.

If their previously unreachable and cold partner, becomes warm, accepting, and loving, their subconscious motivation is affirmed. However, having met the challenge, the codependent loses interest, and ends the relationship, moving on to the next challenge.

On other hand, if they continue to represent a challenge, the relationship continues as the codependent continues their struggle to obtain warm, accepting, and loving behavior from their partner. At a deeper level, we often find that a person who struggled to receive love and attention in childhood, continues the struggle in his adult life.

17.2. The pursuit of ideal love

The subconscious motives of the *inner child* vary. Codependent individuals choose someone problematic who demands that they constantly help them to solve their problems. Their *inner child* believes that only when it is beneficial to someone else, do they deserve to think they are worthy to be loved. This *inner child* does not know the difference between partner love and parental love. For this reason, they have subconscious expectations of their partner, either to adore them in the way their parents did, or to provide them the parental love they did not receive in childhood.

What is the solution for those who move from one unsatisfactory relationship to another, or for those who persist in an unsatisfactory relationship? Step one—stop waiting for the ideal partner who will bring them true love, because change does not come from the outside. Step two—understand your logic in choosing your partner, and from where does it come.

Step three—come to an agreement with yourself, that is to say, resolve the conflict between your rational self and the unreasonable *inner child*. It is crucial that you learn that you deserve to love and be loved.

The heart wants what the heart wants. Your personality is not your only characteristic, is it the only reason the codependent chose you. Keep this in mind—no one knows who you are until you show them, right? So, at some point, you allowed a codependent person to get to know you better. But as I said, regarding love, there is so much more than personality. Your charisma, your beauty...you must keep in mind that codependent person is not a monster. That person is like everyone else, so when it comes to love and relationships, you must be aware that all relationships are a two-way street. You also choose that person, right?

CHAPTER THREE: HOW TO SPEAK
TO A CODEPENDENCY

18.1. Breaking the stereotypes

Let's begin with one stereotype. After years of studying codependency, widespread opinion persists that codependent people are on the margins of our society. However, as far back as the fifties, most codependent persons were found to have family, to be employed, and to have friends. Many could be found in the upper classes and professional fields.

A significant number of mentally ill patients have a family member that suffers from a similar condition. Clinical psychologists and psychiatrists believe that codependency's most devastating consequences are felt by their family. Therefore, we need to be aware that codependency is not only an issue for the codependent, but these issues extend to their family, and shapes relationships among its members. Therefore, it must be treated within the family.

18.2. Why is codependency a family problem?

To make this clear, we will start from the beginning—from the very sign of problems in the codependent's family. The first casualty of code-pendence is communication between spouses. Namely, when one partner notices their spouse acting strangely, particularly by making accusations designed to control the partner. Due to constant criticism, the codependent avoids conversations, lies, and channel the conversation to other topics, pretending not to understand what is being asked, or quickly ending the conversation. This affects the emotional and sexual aspects of the relation-ship, which then becomes unstable, resulting in a complete break in sexual relations and/or marital fidelity, giving rise to jealousy.

Further, this may lead to substitutions in family roles. For example, if the father is codependent, the oldest male child may take on his role, assisting his mother with shopping, bringing his younger siblings to and from school, or attend a parent meeting because dad is at work. Codependency also leads to financial problems, because there may be drug or alcohol addiction problems. This may require the older child to get a job to help financially support the family.

18.3. Why should all family members participate in the treatment of codependency?

From the foregoing, we can see, then, that codependency changes relationships among all family members, and, over time, leads to new patterns of behavior and roles, which further exacerbates family issues. Accordingly, when a codependent has completed treatment and returns to this altered family environment, the family must once more adapt to new conditions. To illustrate the challenges the codependent and their family continues to face, post treatment, I offer this example. Imagine the codependent husband returning from a day's work, tired and annoyed. He finds his wife napping in the armchair, surrounded by a room full of clutter. He begins yelling at her, accusing her of being lazy, although she isn't. She apologizes and explains that she was tired, and therefore, didn't clean the house. However, he doesn't trust her explanation and angrily leaves the house. As a result of this unpleasant event, the ex-codependent risks a return to showing aggression, a trigger that must be avoided. In short, a family in which relationships remain broken, can only survive with mutual respect and understanding. This is the reason it is important to support and treat a family member who is suffering or recovering from the codependent condition. First of all, family must trust them, and demonstrate that they are still needed in the family. Otherwise, they may not feel that their efforts to cure themselves have been fruitful, and they may fear that their loved ones will continue to blame and dismiss them.

18.4. How can a family be cured?

It is extremely difficult to persuade the codependent's family members that the codependent can be cured. After years of trying, asking, broken promises and intermittent recoveries, it is understandable that the family will ask, is healing at all possible? The answer is, yes, of course.

Healing is possible with tremendous effort, patience and dedication. When a codependent enters therapy, other family members must also be involved in the healing process, to provide support to the codependent, to show them that they are important, but also to learn more about their problem and how to deal with it.

It is necessary, from the beginning, to adapt to the new situation that results after their cure. Learn new behaviors and taking on new family roles is part of the process. The codependent needs encouragement in facing their past, accepting reality, and starting their new life. Families also a need to learn how to respond appropriately if signs of the condition re-surface in the codependent. The appropriate response, would be to ensure that they receive regular check-ups with their therapist. Most importantly, don't give up! If a problem arises, the former codependent must receive help to overcome the crisis, without being accused and vilified. Everyone in the family must work to change themselves because the family is a team, and each team member has a role to play.

CHAPTER FOUR: CODEPENDENT RELATIONSHIPS - BEING IN A RELATIONSHIP WITH SOMEONE WITH CODEPENDENCY

People have relationship crises because their expectations for a relationship are generally unrealistic. As we've said before, connections made between the partners are almost always made at the sub-conscious level. Such a crisis is defined as a brief psychic disturbance that, from time to time, occurs in people struggling with life problems that exceed their capacity to cope. The crisis appears as a function disorder in the cognitive, emotional and behavioral plane. On the cognitive plane, it manifests through ego dysfunction, intellectual inefficiency, disrupted concentration, and reasoning, while on the emotional plane there is fear of abandonment, sleep disorders, altered sex drives, and eating disorders.

There are often problems in the relationship that partners can resolve without the help of an expert, but there are also problems that require the help of the expert or psychotherapist. Even couples that have successfully overcome serious problems, may encounter problems such as codependency, when they begin to critically examine their choice of a partner in their relationship. In assessing one's emotional life, a person will compare previous expectations with what is happening in the present, and if expectations are not met, there is a problem with the relationship.

19.1. How to solve a relationship crisis caused by codependency?

Daily communication between partners plays a very important role in the partnership. It is essential for the couple that both parties be able speak and express emotions. All couples should make an effort to understand and respect one another, and to nurture common values. It is necessary to develop empathy, respect, and tolerance. Partners need to define the problems in the relationship and offer solutions. Placing the blame on one another is a significant problem relationship, and leads to additional conflict. Avoiding problems, and postponing communications, also deepen the conflict. So, one should talk about the problem, not run away from it. The cornerstone of a quality partnership is the belief that their partner is worthy of respect and appreciation.

19.2. Does affective attachment style affect the quality of the partnership?

Philosophers, psychologists, and writers have all tried their hand at addressing the question of what people want in a partnership. Nietzsche claimed that a man wants two things—danger and play. Freud concluded that women do not know what they want, but these explanations do not answer the question. There should be moments in each person's life to contemplate what they want in a partner, and what level of emotional connection is the ideal. The qualities of a partnership depend on many factors, such as intimate interactions, loyalty, communication, relationship satisfaction, sexual satisfaction, support, etc. An emotional partner is concurrently the primary provider and recipient of emotional support, a sexual partner, and an affective figure, meaning that depending on the affective pattern formed, the partners will exhibit a degree of care and sexuality.

Affective attachment is manifested differently in codependent people, so in a partner relationship, there are individual differences that are determined by the pattern of affective attachment. Kim Bartolomeu talked about four styles of attachment, 1) safe, 2) preoccupied, 3) timid, and 4) dismissive. *Safe* individuals build open and authentic partnerships, have high self-confidence, easily achieve intimacy in relationships, and constructively resolve conflicts. For people with this pattern of affective attach-

ment, emotional intercourse with others is very important, and in the partnership, they are securely attached because, in addition to feeling self-
worth, they enjoy the closeness and intimacy.

On the other hand, codependent persons are dependent on partners, invest too much in a partnership, and have the belief that they *must* be loved.
These persons are territorial in representing their love and idealizing their
partner. Afflicted persons have a conflict of motives, seek affirmation of
their personal values from their partners, and they are passive and dependent. Chaos is the major feature of their relationships. The avoid bonding
with people that are compulsively self-reliant, superior, and have an increased need for autonomy. They build short-term and superficial connections. Lack of closeness, intimacy, and expression of emotions are their
characteristics. They have the conviction that the relationship suffocates,
but the root of the fear is rejection.

Various world-wide studies show that securely bonded couples work
better together, are more satisfied in the relationship, and constructively
resolve conflicts. According to behavioral theory, compatible partner behaviors lead to higher quality partnerships.

19.3. Same or different styles of attachment

Research shows that dyads, in which both members have a secure attachment style, are of better quality. The same behavioral system and emotional response, the experience of acceptance, support, availability, and
sensitivity of the partners lead to these couples having a good relationship.
Couples in which the dyad members are differently related, are likely to
rate their relationship as lower quality, due to differences in the behavioral,
cognitive, and emotional systems. One member who suffers from codependency may have a high level of anxiety accompanied by fear of abandonment, while the other may have a low level of anxiety accompanied by
an experience of self-worth. The same rule applies to the avoidance do-
main. One partner may express and accept trust, and closeness, the other

may be distrustful and disinterested in expressing closeness. These differences lead to frequent marital conflicts, dissatisfaction, misunderstandings, and inconsistencies, which have detrimental effects on the quality of marriage. Married couples who share the same levels of anxiety and avoidance, will have a higher quality relationship than couples having disparate levels of anxiety and avoidance.

19.4. Relationship with a codependent person

You have been in an emotional relationship for a long time and everything seems to be fine. Your partner is fully committed, and you feel loved. However, that doesn't make you happy. You have the feeling that you have lost yourself. You cannot distinguish your wants, from your partner's needs. You are chronically dissatisfied, even depressed. You feel like you are in a cage, and as though you are no longer you. These signals can indicate that you are in a symbiotic emotional relationship.

19.5. What is a symbiotic emotional relationship?

The term symbiotic relationship is commonly used to describe the type of relationship that occurs in an animal species. It is a relationship in which two individuals interact with each other for their common benefit. These individuals are functionally and physically connected, and operate as one organism. In humans, the symbiotic relationship is the fusion of two people into one, meaning they cannot function effectively without each other. Practically speaking, *you and me* become *we*, a new plane of existence in which both persons lose their individuality. This kind of relationship is not exclusive to partners in a relationship or marriage, it may also be present in relationships with friends, or parent-child relationships.

19.6. What kinds of persons are inclined to build symbiotic relationships?

Although relationships between partners imply equality, it is possible for one person to be drawn into a symbiotic relationship by the other. Usually, this happens under the guise of *true love*, that is to say, one of the partners involved is very happy, because they have received unconditional love and commitment from the other partner. It is important to understand that a symbiotic relationship is completely normal in the early stage of a relationship and can last for several months. The partners are in a state of falling in love, so, they feel like one being. They are oblivious to those around them. Still, this is just a phase, and should by no means persist long-term.

People who build purely symbiotic emotional relationships have a fear of being left behind/rejected. Usually, such persons have had very painful experiences in their lives. Experiences in primary family relationships or previous partnerships (because of the condition they suffer) that they want to avoid repeating at all costs. To ensure that such experiences are not repeated, they fully commit to their partner and demand that they do so in return. Also, the person tries to compensate for emotional losses that occurred in previous relationships by intensifying the current one, which results in a hunger for constant attention and closeness. These are generally addictive personality types that cannot function on their own, and seek a strong, supportive figure in another person. These kinds of people have the philosophy that, "If I'm not with someone I'm not worthy", "I need another person to feel complete", "Life without the love and attention of another person is not a life" and so on.

19.7. What are the signs that you are in a symbiotic emotional relationship?

As I've outlined above, a person who is involved in a symbiotic relationship may feel loved and special, at first, and then a covert depression occurs, although, outwardly, everything is okay. Yet the person is unhappy, lost, feeling that they are losing themselves. Moreover, all social aspects of life are neglected—contact with friends is lost. In a healthy relationship, it is normal that you will share the bulk of your time with your partner, and that you will rarely see your friends. This is a matter of gradually eliminating old friendships, while, at the same time, forming new friendships that include your partner. However, in symbiotic relationships, you don't make new friendships, especially not with the opposite sex (e.g. colleague/colleague at work) as these will be misinterpreted. As a result, your social circle shrinks and you are "doomed" to contact with only one person. Personal interests, desires and goals are reduced or extinguished. In spending more time with your partner, you will neglect your hobbies, interests, activities, and professional development. Even though you realize that something is wrong, you still feel guilty because if they could give up their interests, hobbies, professional challenges, and social circle, how can you not do the same.

Convinced that you have found your *true love* you make the decision to devote yourself completely to one person, because they alone deserve it. A symbiotic relationship is *not* a healthy relationship between two people. When you assess that you are not progressing with your partner on a personal plane, when you realize that your social life is completely shut down, when you feel unhappy, and depressed, consider whether it is time to change things in your relationship, set boundaries, and fight for your individuality.

CHAPTER FIVE: HEALTHY RELATIONSHIPS/ BOUNDARIES

All of us want to have happiness in love. Many of us think that we need to be born under a lucky star to have a healthy emotional connection. That's just not true.

Healthy emotional relationships can be learned, just like everything else in life. Some of us have had the benefit of positive role models in as we were growing up, and we passively and effortlessly adopted healthy behaviors. Others, who had no such opportunity, nonetheless possess all the potential and all the qualities necessary to create a healthy and fulfilling relationship.

20.1. Immature love

Immature love follows the principle, "I love because I am loved." In contrast, mature love follows the principle, "I am loved because I love." Immature love says, "I love you because you need me," and mature love allows for independence and free expression of ideas and feelings. It discusses values and encourages expression.

Elements of addiction also exist in most mature relationships. We can recognize and accept them, unravel the myths that support them, do what we can to change them, and thus achieve the healthy aspects of the relationship. How do we know that our love is an addiction?

20.2. Characteristics of addictive love

People in addictive relationships have the following characteristics:

1. They routinely feel exhausted
2. They cannot define ego boundaries

3. They exhibit sadomasochism
4. They are afraid to let things run their course
5. They are afraid of risk, change, and the unknown
6. Have a small shift in personal growth
7. They have no experience of true closeness
8. They play psychological games
9. They want to mold their partner
10. They need their partner to feel complete
11. They seek and demand unconditional love
12. They relive old, negative feelings

20.3. Characteristics of healthy love

People in a healthy relationship have the following characteristics:

1. They allow self-sufficiency
2. They share the same experience—that they are one with their partner, and they are each for themselves
3. They encourage the best in their partner
4. They accept endings
5. They are opened to change and exploration
6. They encourage personal growth in their partner
7. They experience true closeness
8. They feel free to seek what they need
9. They feel that giving and receiving are equally important
10. They have no intention of diminishing or controlling another
11. They encourage self-sufficiency in their partner
12. They accept their partner's boundaries
13. They do not seek unconditional love
14. They are self-confident

Of course, everyone wants their relationship to be normal and perfect, but most don't really know what that looks like. Here are some guidelines on how healthy relationships should look.

20.4. You have realistic expectations from love

I hope that you are aware that perfection does not exist, and that your partner cannot be perfect. Perfection exists in those small imperfections that make the connection beautiful and sweet. It is very important in to accept not only your flaws, but also your partner's flaws and turn them into something bearable and even sweet. When you love someone, those things that would usually annoy you become sweet and cute.

20.5. Do not take everything personally

Instead of blaming your partner for everything they do wrong, you should discuss them, until these things are resolved to the mutual satisfaction of both partners. Don't take everything personally. People are constantly being wronged. Your partner did not intentionally do something wrong, things happen.

20.6. You are a team

Together, you can accomplish whatever you want. Remember that you should not compete, but revel in each other's victories. Relationships are not a competitive sport, so, accept that you share the same goals and work together to resolve your problems.

20.7. Trust and compromise

It is very important that in each relationship, the partners can find mutual pursuits that both parties will enjoy. There is no need for quarrels because you are one soul and two bodies, that's something to remember when there are quarrels between you. Also very important, is the confidence you build in one another. A relationship becomes stronger and more stable when you can trust the person you are in a relationship with. This must be established between you.

20.8. Discussion

It is important to have honest conversations between partners in a relationship or marriage. Each problem can be solved with the strength of two people who can honestly express their opinions. You need to express your likes and dislikes. Many people want to live according to spiritual ideals, such as helping others, kindness, generosity, sharing, etc. In many books, you will read about the ideal behavior that we should strive for. These are learned patterns that were implanted in our childhood. Rarely does a family fail to teach their child that they should share with others, be good, and be obedient. This implicitly indicates to the child that everything will be okay if they put others before themselves. Obedience has always been valued above individuality.

20.9. The main problem

The problem arises because we forget that most people are still at a rather low level of emotional maturity and awareness regarding relationships. Many people are clueless on how to respect the personal boundaries of others. Others will consciously take advantage of a perceived weakness in another person. As you can see, a person who tries to be kind and helpful to others can quickly find themselves in situations that are exhausting, because people constantly take advantage of them. There is no joy in such relationships. Yet kind and helpful people do all they can meet these expectations at the expense of their own feelings, which leads to frustration and anger. Not only is frustration and anger considered socially undesirable, but a person who satisfies others at their own expense, often feel tremendous discomfort with the anger and frustration that they have, so, they suppress it.

20.10. Spending yourself out of decency

If you find yourself in this situation, you must know that you owe no one your time, love, or friendship. These are abstract categories for which we rarely consider how to set boundaries, that is, what we want and what we don't want. In this area, we may feel guiltier than in other areas, such as the amount of money we spend. Our parents probably didn't give out a lot of money, but many children watched their parents spend time and energy on people they didn't want to be with, so as not to not offend them. In this way, indirectly, and sometimes directly, we learned to act the same.

Sometimes the best way to help someone is to turn them away, to not allow them to *hang* on us, and consume our time and energy. In this way, we actually help the person learn to cope, by handling their own needs, relying on their own strengths and develop independence. Intervention would only increase their dependence. We are not usually aware of these dynamics, and we fail to realize that our outreach may do more harm than good. We've all heard the old saying, the road to hell is paved with good intentions.

Even if you do not find anything negative in the other person, they may they may not be attractive to you as a potential friend. There is nothing wrong with that, and there is no reason to feel guilty for rejecting the friendship offered. Not all people are made to be a part of our lives, and that's fine.

20.11. The feelings of others

Mature, quality communication does not always have to be an effort designed to make your partner feel good or to avoid hurting their feelings. This, of course, does not mean that we should hurt others recklessly on the pretext of doing so for their own good. We must have boundaries in everything, and that's exactly what I'm writing about here. Often, when we avoid telling someone directly what we think, we are just avoiding the problem. The other person will remain unaware of the problem and continue to cross our boundary. Eventually the situation devolves into open conflict or avoidance, both of which leave a bitter taste.

The basic rule is that you are responsible for your behavior, but not for the other person's feelings. So, if you have done your best to communicate, shown them respect, and maintained your integrity, there is no reason to feel guilty, even if the other person feels hurt.

20.12. Establishing boundaries

If one partner denies the other partner's desire or request, or sets boundaries that are not suitable for the other partner, the other partner may consider modifying their requirements in order to maintain the relationship, or perhaps change the form or intensity of the relationship, and seek what they want in another relationship. All this can be done without harm and blame, as a natural process, if we perceive each other as equals with equal needs. What is essential is that we communicate it. But if the other partner does not see you for who you are, and instead projects upon you their expectations of a parent, partner or child, they will feel hurt, disappointed, and make their happiness and feelings dependent on your behavior, which is a recipe for suffering.

In any communication with someone more important than a casual acquaintance, it is good to clarify what each of the parties wants and whether that is acceptable to the other, especially if we see that the expectations are different. We cannot expect the other person to be automatically obliged to consent to something because we want it, or want the same form of relationship. We are all personalities unto ourselves and we are all different, no matter how similar we may be. This is what makes us human and this is what gives us the potential for happiness. How many unhappy people would there be in the world, if we all wanted the same things?

20.13. Boundaries in partnerships

Setting boundaries is just as important in a partnership as in any other relationship. In this area, partners also, have exaggerated expectations and needs from their partner. I could repeat everything I've written earlier on the subject, but just know that it applies equally to partnerships

20.14. Responses to border violations

How do we recognize what our borders are and when they are not respected? This is where the usual advice should be repeated. Observe the subtle emotions and try to translate them into words as best you can. If your emotions do not alert you strongly enough, eventually your physical body may start alerting you.

If we notice that one is encroaching our boundaries, it is not a reason to place ourselves in an offensive or defensive stance, or to demonstrate righteous anger. Anger and blame are just signs of our repressed fear and unresolved guilt. Of course that needs to be acknowledged and explored. It is necessary to learn the difference between determination and defense, as well as the difference between yielding and compassion. This may be difficult at first, because we have all learned, to suppress our needs and alter our boundaries. That is why we usually react with guilt, fear, and anger when we are forced to set or reset them, which usually occurs only following a period of ingestion, indulgence, and accumulated feelings of discomfort.

Some people defend their borders very firmly, and very aggressively, blaming others for small things. They also essentially respond out of fear and guilt, but these feelings are much less accessible to the conscious mind. Such individuals were likely to have been injured in childhood, so they learned to fight for themselves. The problem starts with their, "I'll hurt you before you hurt me" attitude. That attitude essentially reflects their fear, and their insecurity. Such a person does not understand that they can protect themselves and take care of themselves without directly attacking and belittling others. It is not a display of self-esteem, but rather just another iteration of the same problem.

Assuming, with the exception of direct aggression or manipulation, that people do not act with a conscious intention to hurt or exploit us, but simply out of an underdeveloped awareness of other people's values and feelings, there is no reason to react with anger. If we react with anger, we may sabotage a relationship that has the potential to be of good quality.

It is crucial to recognize, define and explain our boundaries, needs, and desires at the earliest possible stage of any relationship we have with other persons. We must do this before dissatisfaction builds. The problem, is that we have not learned to pay attention to the messages of our emotions and our bodies, and react to those messages quickly. This frequently results in an emotional, sometimes physical crisis, which result from our failure to react.

Be aware of these message, and then calmly, without fear, guilt, or anger, explain to the other person what you want or what you disagree with. To the extent that you are unable to, you will feel uncomfortable and anxious in contact with that person, which is why we usually attribute the blame to them and not to ourselves. We must understand that just as we do not respect ourselves and our needs, we frequently do not respect them and their needs, even if it is only in our minds.

It is important to understand that if you feel uncomfortable in your interactions with a person, it is likely that one of you has been unable to set boundaries that the other will be able to respect. Certainly, some people simply dislike us, and cannot be friends with us for some objective or subjective reason. However, if this is not the case, then it is likely that there is a problem in establishing boundaries. For example, the person may be taking more than they are giving. That's why it's important to set boundaries. It will benefit you and, most importantly, others interacting with you.

CHAPTER SIX: WHAT TO DO WHEN YOUR LOVE HAS CODEPENDENCY

It's not easy to watch a loved one struggle with codependency, and in most cases, people don't know how to put themselves in that situation. Here are some tips to teach you how to help your partner with their codependent condition. Although sadness is an integral part of life, if you notice that your partner is going through a period of intense feelings of sadness that last for more than a few days, these may be the first signs of the codependent condition. There are several things you can do to help yourself and your partner more easily push through that challenging period for both of you.

21.1. How to identify symptoms of codependency in your partner

Do not take these symptoms as a rule, as symptoms of codependency can vary from person to person. The most common symptoms include feelings of sadness that lasts at least two weeks, loss of interest in hobbies, friends, sex, eating disorders, sleeping disorders, nervousness, hopelessness, helplessness, feelings of worthlessness, sudden outbursts of anger, constant expressions of criticism, and/or suicidal thoughts.

21.2. Encourage your partner to seek help

Codependency can be so debilitating that the individual becomes incapable of seeking help, and many of those who are codependent are ashamed of their condition. If you suspect that your loved one is suffering from this condition, I suggest that you consult an expert. Schedule an appointment with a psychiatrist who will make the right assessment and be sure to ask your partner if they want you to go for moral support. If your partner refuses to see a doctor, consult a specialist about the following steps.

21.3. Educate yourself

The more you learn about codependency, its symptoms, its impact, and how it is treated, the easier it will be to understand what your partner is going through, and the easier it will be to help them make important decisions about their treatment. Ask questions, read books, and consult an expert. Talk to your partner's doctor about anything you need to learn about.

21.4. Talk

Encourage your partner to open up to tell you all the most hidden thoughts that pop into their head. Having a serious and honest conversation about their feelings will make it known that you care, that you take them seriously, and that you will, in some way, bring them relief. Avoid complicated topics, stick to simple words, and do not condemn. Listen—listen carefully to everything your partner has to say, be careful not to interrupt them and never finish their sentences.

21.5. Participate in the repair

Although you may not understand the reasons for your partner's condition, you must support them during the recovery process. Make sure they take their medication regularly, accompany them to their psychiatrist's sessions, but only if they want you to. Try to prevent situations that could cause them anxiety, fear, or stress. This means that you may be compelled to take on some of the obligations that your partner had been responsible for, such as paying bills, and arguing with neighbors.

21.6. Give your partner hope

Hope comes in many different forms, some find it through faith, others through their children. Discover your partner's greatest hope and remind them of that hope when they think everything is lost. Make sure you are there for them all the time.

21.7. Identify warning signs

Codependent people often have suicidal tendencies when they can no longer cope with feelings of hopelessness and helplessness. If your partner starts mentioning suicide, take it seriously and don't assume they won't put their thoughts into action.

21.8. Take care of yourself

At times, when we care for a loved one, it can be very easy for us to neglect ourselves and our needs, but you must keep in mind that if you are unable to function normally, you will not be able to help your partner. Feelings of depression can easily pass on to you as well. Make sure you eat well, sleep well, exercise, and keep in touch with family and friends who can support you if needed. Take time for yourself and look at the situation from a distance. Consider joining psychotherapy yourself or joining forums to connect with people who are going through the same thing.

CHAPTER SEVEN: BREAKING UP WITH SOMEONE WHO HAS CODEPENDENCY – WHEN IS THE TIME TO END IT?

If you are questioning whether to leave, or give your relationship another chance, perhaps this will help you decide. There are ups and downs in every relationship, but the way we overcome bad times says a lot about whether or not that love has a future. If the person suffering from this condition does not want to be treated, or does not acknowledge the problem, then it is time to end the relationship. If you don't do this, you will waste your life in vain—remember that. You cannot expect someone to be there for you if you are not prepared to do the same for them.

If you are questioning whether to leave or give your relationship another chance, perhaps this will inform your decision.

22.1. Some obvious signs that your relationship is not going to be saved

- You know deep inside that you are not happy

If you feel that way, you are wasting your time. The question of whether you are happy or not is not subject to compromise.

- You are no longer close to your partner

If you've moved on, and if you feel that it's irreversible, you're probably right. There's no point in continuing to suffer. End the relationship.

- You don't see a common future

If you can't imagine yourself together in the future. If all your plans and dreams are yours, and yours alone, why would you stay in that relationship?

- You feel like you're pretending all the time

It is as if your true nature is *on hold,* because you can no longer express it in this relationship.

- You would do anything rather than spend time with your partner

If you stay longer at work than you need to, if you make up a thousand reasons to stay in the city, just because you don't want to go home, then...go. It is not fair neither to you nor to your partner, to remain in the relationship.

- You no longer choose your words

If you find yourself increasingly uncomfortable with their comments, if you are being unkind, if you don't have the patience to say something nice, why would you continue a toxic relationship?

- It everything your partner does or says gets on your nerves

When the most banal of conversations sets your hair afire, when you can't stand the way she sits on the bed before she goes to sleep, when you get angry if she leaves her sneakers where she always leaves them, when you suddenly notice that she washes the dishes slowly, and you realize that this is not the person you fell in love with. You have changed, your love is gone, and it is much better for you to leave, rather than spend your life being angry and anxious.

- You are aware that the only reason you are still together is your fear of being alone

That's so pathetic—if there is no love, go. Don't ruin the life of someone you once loved because of your fears.

- You can no longer talk without arguing

Not even agreeing on what to have dinner, or where to go for the week-end turns into a fight. Communication is one of the most important things in a relationship. But if only contempt remains, instead of love, then why frown? And more importantly, why blame the person you used to love. Go!

- When you need solace, you do not seek it from your partner

In a loving relationship your partner is a safe harbor. If you don't have that any longer, just go.

- You have nothing in common anymore

Have you moved so far that you can no longer watch TV together, be-cause you are interested in completely different topics? It is time to let go.

The bottom line and the simple message is this: If you have tried eve-rything and found no solution—end the relationship. You have only one life, and no one, that you do not love, is worthy to take your life.

CHAPTER EIGHT: HOW TO FIX BROKEN RELATIONSHIPS

I honestly believe that any relationship that is broken due to this condition can be repaired. This condition is to blame for all the bad things that have happened in all of their relationships. The person who suffers from this condition is always understood to be the culprit. Now, with new knowledge, relationships can be easily repaired if there is mutual understanding and appreciation.

Here, everyone must know that compromise is important. Everyone has to understand the other side.

Understanding is the key. If there is an understanding, the relationship will be repaired and if there isn't an understanding, it cannot be repaired. Forgiveness and understanding are the keys to repairing all relationships.

23.1. Forgiveness

First of all, everyone is hurt as a consequence of this condition. So, the most important thing, is to learn how to forgive.

This condition is very specific and very serious. It can cause a great deal of damage to a relationship. There is no more to say when it comes to this.

23.2. How to forgive

Everyone involved in this vicious circle has suffered greatly, and that is a fact. However, if you read carefully you have learned that the codependent person is also a victim of this condition. So you must understand that everything that has transpired is a consequence of this condition. So open your heart, and look deep into yourself. Is there an element of intent that caused all of this? There is no element of intent. The person who hurt you couldn't comprehend doing that to you. The condition is the cause of your disagreements. The codependent is not the guilty party in this. You must have this in mind when you are deciding if will you forgive that person. Forgiveness is our nature, so, try to put yourself in the position of this person. How would you feel about forgiving then? You must be objective, and I believe that everyone deserves a second chance. That is still the same person you once loved. Give it a try, that person deserves that much.

23.3. Try to understand the problem

Nowadays, everyone is very busy, and not many people will make the time to deal with others. Everyone is living in the fast lane. But, stop and think about what you are doing. Try to understand that there will be a time, later in your life, when you will need someone to pick you up. Every one of us has that moment in their life when they need someone. Now, you can make a good decision, and you can choose to understand the importance of helping, and letting the past go.

23.4. Think about tomorrow

Many people are stuck in the past and they are unable to let go of all that has happened. Try to focus on tomorrow. Before you cross off someone from your life, think twice about it. There is a good chance that you will lose much more than you will gain.

CHAPTER NINE: HOW TO HELP
SOMEONE CODEPENDENT?

This will be a very short chapter because the message in this is simple. You have everything you need in previous chapters, and all that you need to help someone who has a codependency condition, is your personal will.

Your will is essential.

We have all done something that we know is not good for us. Do we have a weak will?

Although the will is based on desire, it is important to distinguish it from desire. Desire is one of many emotions. To feel desire is to be motivated to the actions that lead to its realization. This kind of motivation lasts as long as the person feels their desire. The problem with emotions in general, and even with desires, is that they are transient. One can feel desire for days or weeks and then, in a moment it's gone. Then we lose our motivation as well. This is a pattern of behavior is typical of unsuccessful people, they get excited about something, are inspired by it for a time, lose their motivation for a moment, and give up the whole thing entirely, or postpone it to some future time.

It is not good when a person is motivated only by feelings or the principle of seeking the pleasant, and avoiding the unpleasant. Personality is a complex system, all parts of which should govern behavior. The ability of a person move toward their desired goals is called *will*. It is a higher form of motivation, important for the achievement of goals that are not at your fingertips, but which must be pursued vigorously over time.

So, your *will* and your desire are crucial, and in addition to your *will* and your desire, this book has taught you everything you need to know in order to help someone who is suffering from the codependent condition.

CONCLUSION

Dear readers, I believe that we managed to achieve our task in this book. We went very deep to reveal this condition for everyone interested in knowing it better. I believe that we managed to send a message. We talked about this condition, we defined codependent disorder, we explained what a codependent person is, we point out specific therapies and symptoms of the condition, and we went through the main reasons for this condition thoroughly. My goal was to show the readers the seriousness of this condition and to provide them with concrete evidence that this condition is one that can be cured. I believe that I have completed my task. My message for codependents is unchanged: Yes, you can be better, yes you can "repair your watch", yes you can have a better life and a better future by letting go of the past. You will find yourself again and you will love yourself again. Why am I saying that? Because I know that in every one of us there is a fighter—a warrior. This is your battle, and it is also your life. Don't waste your life and the lives of your loved ones. You have only one life; make the most of that life.

Don't be your enemy, be your best friend—believe in yourself. Use your time wisely, read this book and you will have a good and normal life, the life you've been seeking since you were born.

You are a watchmaker, learn how to find the missing part of your watch...

Please tell me what you think of the information you've read. Leave a review. I hope this has been helpful.